DATE DUE			

Understanding
American History

The Great Depression

Linda and Charles George

Bruno Leone
Series Consultant

ReferencePoint
Press®

San Diego, CA

© 2013 ReferencePoint Press, Inc.
Printed in the United States

For more information, contact:
ReferencePoint Press, Inc.
PO Box 27779
San Diego, CA 92198
www. ReferencePointPress.com

LIBRARY OF CONGRESS CATALOGING-IN-PUBLICATION DATA

George, Linda.
  The Great Depression : part of the understanding American history series / by Linda and Charles George.
    p. cm. -- (Understanding American history)
  Includes bibliographical references and index.
  ISBN-13: 978-1-60152-492-8 (hardback)
  ISBN-10: 1-60152-492-7 (hardback)
  1. Depressions--1929--United States--Juvenile literature. 2. United States--History--1933-1945--Juvenile literature. 3. United States--History--1919-1933--Juvenile literature. 4. New Deal, 1933-1939--Juvenile literature. 5. United States--Economic conditions--1918-1945--Juvenile literature. I. George, Charles, 1949- II. Title.
  E806.G467 2013
  973.916--dc23
                                                                    2012032156

Contents

Foreword

America's Puritan ancestors—convinced that their adopted country was blessed by God and would eventually rise to worldwide prominence—proclaimed their new homeland the shining "city upon a hill." The nation that developed since those first hopeful words were uttered has clearly achieved prominence on the world stage and it has had many shining moments but its history is not without flaws. The history of the United States is a virtual patchwork of achievements and blemishes. For example, America was originally founded as a New World haven from the tyranny and persecution prevalent in many parts of the Old World. Yet the colonial and federal governments in America took little or no action against the use of slave labor by the southern states until the 1860s, when a civil war was fought to eliminate slavery and preserve the federal union.

In the decades before and after the Civil War, the United States underwent a period of massive territorial expansion; through a combination of purchase, annexation, and war, its east–west borders stretched from the Atlantic to the Pacific Oceans. During this time, the Industrial Revolution that began in eighteenth-century Europe found its way to America, where it was responsible for considerable growth of the national economy. The United States was now proudly able to take its place in the Western Hemisphere's community of nations as a worthy economic and technological partner. Yet America also chose to join the major western European powers in a race to acquire colonial empires in Africa, Asia, and the islands of the Caribbean and South Pacific. In this scramble for empire, foreign territories were often peacefully annexed but military force was readily used when needed, as in the Philippines during the Spanish-American War of 1898.

Toward the end of the nineteenth century and concurrent with America's ambitions to acquire colonies, its vast frontier and expanding industrial base provided both land and jobs for a new and ever-growing wave of immigrants from southern and eastern Europe. Although America had always encouraged immigration, these newcomers—Italians, Greeks, and eastern European Jews, among others—were seen as different from the vast majority of earlier immigrants, most of whom were from northern and western Europe. The presence of these newcomers was treated as a matter of growing concern, which in time evolved into intense opposition. Congress boldly and with calculated prejudice set out to create a barrier to curtail the influx of unwanted nationalities and ethnic groups to America's shores. The outcome was the National Origins Act, passed in 1924. That law severely reduced immigration to the United States from southern and eastern Europe. Ironically, while this was happening, the Statue of Liberty stood in New York Harbor as a visible and symbolic beacon lighting the way for people of *all* nationalities and ethnicities seeking sanctuary in America.

Unquestionably, the history of the United States has not always mirrored that radiant beacon touted by the early settlers. As often happens, reality and dreams tend to move in divergent directions. However, the story of America also reveals a people who have frequently extended a helping hand to a weary world and who have displayed a ready willingness—supported by a flexible federal constitution—to take deliberate and effective steps to correct injustices, past and present. America's private and public philanthropy directed toward other countries during times of natural disasters (such as the contributions of financial and human resources to assist Haiti following the January 2010 earthquake) and the legal right to adopt amendments to the US Constitution (including the Thirteenth Amendment freeing the slaves and the Nineteenth Amendment granting women the right to vote) are examples of the nation's generosity and willingness to acknowledge and reverse wrongs.

With objectivity and candor, the titles selected for the Understanding American History series portray the many sides of America, depicting both its shining moments and its darker hours. The series strives to help readers achieve a wider understanding and appreciation of the American experience and to encourage further investigation into America's evolving character and founding principles.

Important Events of the
Great Depression

1929
The stock market crashes on October 29, leading to the worst economic depression in US and world history.

1931
Extreme drought hits the midwestern and southern plains, causing severe dust storms; 2,293 US banks suspend operations.

1923
President Harding dies on August 2; Vice President Calvin Coolidge is sworn in as president on August 3, ushering in an era that came to be known as Coolidge Prosperity.

| 1920 | 1927 | 1929 | 1931 | 1933 |

1928
Herbert Hoover is elected president on November 6.

1930
The Smoot-Hawley Tariff Act is signed into law on June 17, raising tariffs on over twenty thousand imported goods.

1920
Americans hear the first radio broadcast; radio will become an essential form of communication during the Great Depression. Warren G. Harding is elected president on November 2.

1932
Democrat Franklin Delano Roosevelt (FDR) is elected president on November 8, defeating Republican Herbert Hoover's bid for a second term.

1933
The First Hundred Days of FDR's term sees numerous agencies created to stimulate the economy and restore confidence in the banking system; the Twenty-First Amendment is ratified on December 5, repealing Prohibition; the first Civilian Conservation Corps soil erosion camp opens in Alabama.

1937
Roosevelt's Shelterbelt Project begins in March, designed to protect the Great Plains from wind erosion; the US Housing Act is passed on September 1, creating the US Housing Authority and providing low-interest loans to communities.

1938
The Fair Labor Standards Act is passed on June 25, establishing the first minimum wage.

1940
Roosevelt is elected to a third presidential term; the Selective Training and Service Act (the draft) is enacted on September 16, requiring men aged twenty-one to thirty-five to register for possible military duty.

1934
The Securities and Exchange Commission (SEC), charged with regulating Wall Street, is created on June 6.

1935   **1937**   **1939**   **1941**

1939
Germany invades Poland on September 1, beginning World War II.

1935
Extensive damage occurs throughout the Dust Bowl states as a result of the "Black Sunday" storm, which takes place on April 8; the Social Security Act to protect older Americans is passed on August 23.

1941
Japanese forces attack Pearl Harbor, Hawaii, on December 7, prompting the United States to declare war on Japan on December 8; Germany and Italy declare war on the United States on December 11.

1936
Roosevelt is elected to a second term as president.

The Defining Characteristics of the Great Depression

The son of Jewish immigrants from Russia, Yip Harburg lived on the Lower East Side of New York City in the 1930s. In 1932, two and a half years into the Great Depression, he, along with composer Jay Gorney, wrote the song "Brother, Can You Spare a Dime?" In its lyrics, an unemployed American portraying first a construction worker, then a farmer, and finally a soldier stands in a long line, waiting for a handout. He laments that everything he has done to help build and defend his nation seems to have been for naught, since he has been reduced to begging even for a dime to buy a cup of coffee. The song's lyrics expressed what most Americans felt during the Great Depression, and it became so popular that Roosevelt used it as the theme song for his 1932 presidential campaign. The Great Depression—this period of high unemployment, poverty, broken families, low profits, and few opportunities for economic growth and personal advancement—lasted from mid-1929 to late 1941, and its effects struck not only the United States but the entire world.

The emotions most Americans felt during those terrible years were fear and incredulity—anxiety for the future and a general lack of understanding of what had happened to them and to the country they loved. In an interview for the 1970 book *Hard Times: An Oral History of the*

Great Depression, Harburg explains the shock felt by most Americans when the stock market crashed in 1929, ushering in a decade known by most Americans as just "hard times": "We thought American business was the Rock of Gibraltar. We were the prosperous nation, and nothing could stop us now. A brownstone house was forever. You gave it to your kids and they put marble fronts on it. There was a feeling of continuity. If you made it, it was there forever. Suddenly the big dream exploded. The impact was unbelievable."[1]

When asked why he wrote "Brother, Can You Spare a Dime?," Harburg replied that it was a phrase often heard on the streets of New York City during the Depression:

> The prevailing greeting at that time, on every block you passed, by some poor guy coming up, was: "Can you spare a dime?" Or: "Can you spare something for a cup of coffee?" . . . I thought that could be a beautiful title. If I could work it out by telling people, through the song, it isn't just a man asking for a dime. This is the man who says: I built the railroads. I built that tower. I fought your wars. I was the kid with the drum. Why the hell should I be standing in line now? What happened to all this wealth I created?[2]

Fear

Along with feelings of outrage and a lack of understanding came fear. According to American historian T.H. Watkins, "Fear was the great leveler of the Great Depression."[3] No American was untouched when stock prices plummeted on Wall Street, destroying the personal wealth of thousands; when banks closed their doors to depositors, plunging many into bankruptcy; when factories shut down, laying off hundreds of thousands of workers; when farm prices fell to such levels that there were no markets for their goods; and when dust storms hit America's heartland, destroying crops and burying homesteads. Watkins calls it "a terrible, scarring experience that changed this country and its people forever."[4]

Worried account holders congregate outside a New York City bank closed by the state in 1931. The Great Depression led to thousands of bank failures all across the United States and brought financial ruin to workers, business owners, farmers, investors, and families at all income levels.

Even the wealthy, many of whom lived through the period largely untouched, feared the Great Depression. Watkins says, "Even if they did not lose their jobs or go hungry themselves, even if the terror of want passed over them without touching them, most Americans felt its passage like a cold, unforgettable wind."[5]

Depression

According to the website MedicineNet.com, depression is defined as "An illness that involves the body, mood, and thought and that affects the way a person eats, sleeps, feels about himself or herself, and thinks about things. Depression is not the same as a passing blue mood. It is not a sign of personal weakness or a condition that can be wished away."[6] Although this is a definition of the medical condition known as clinical depression, much of it applies to the general feeling of Americans during the era of the Great Depression, as well.

The Great Depression was a decade-long period of economic collapse in the United States and around the world in the 1930s. Overproduction of food and manufactured goods in the United States (producing more than American consumers could purchase), the loss of overseas markets due to the effects of World War I and to high tariffs, and a general spirit of financial and social recklessness in the 1920s began the downward spiral. Once the stock market crashed in late 1929, the end results were closed banks, idle factories, widespread unemployment and poverty, masses of people on the move in search of work and relief, and an overall feeling of defeat and lack of hope.

Chapter 1

What Conditions Led to the Great Depression?

Besides the American Civil War and World War II, no era of American history has been more completely documented or more thoroughly studied than the Great Depression. Despite this intense scrutiny, some historians still disagree as to its root causes and even to its official starting and ending dates. The Great Depression did not begin, as many believe, on the day the New York Stock Exchange crashed—October 29, 1929—nor was the crash the sole cause of the Depression. A part of *The LIFE History of the United States, 1917–1932: Boom and Bust*, explains it this way:

> [The crash] did not really happen on a single day. The structure of the stock market had been unsteady for months, as if some great, elemental force were stirring beneath it. But each time a crack had appeared, somehow it had been covered. Then, late in October 1929, there came a day when the cracks kept on opening until the whole crazy structure fell to pieces. It took a dozen years and the eve of [World War II] to put the economy back together.[7]

The crash was the result of numerous factors, stretching back more than a decade that like threads, became interwoven into an economic knot that seemed impossible to untangle. The first of those threads formed during and immediately after World War I.

Wartime Prosperity

The war that began in Europe in 1914 eventually came to be known as World War I. It lasted four years. Once the United States entered the conflict, the wartime economy that developed from it brought prosperity to the nation, ending a time of national economic recession that had begun in 1907. Since its founding in 1776, the United States had undergone numerous declines in gross domestic product (GDP) that resulted in recession or depression—in 1819, 1837, 1857, 1883, 1907, and 1921. GDP is the total of all goods and services produced within a country during a specific time period. A recession is a slowing of a nation's economy—a decline or leveling off of the GDP—that results in lost jobs. Recessions are relatively common and are determined by how long they last—usually a minimum of six months. A depression is an exceptionally rare event, occurring when an economy gets so bad that the country's GDP drops by more than 10 percent or when a recession has lasted more than two years.

When American production of food, goods, and services to support the Allied troops involved in World War I began in earnest in 1914, the United States experienced wartime prosperity. Farmers enjoyed a boom in demand that brought higher prices, encouraging them to increase their production. Many borrowed money, using their farms as collateral, so they could buy more land and produce more crops. Also benefiting from the war effort were manufacturers of clothing, weapons, and other manufactured goods needed to support the US Army and the armies of American allies in Europe. Jobs in America were plentiful, and wages increased. Morale was high and displays of patriotism frequent; men enlisted in the army, women took over traditionally male factory jobs, and children waved flags in honor of fathers, uncles, and brothers who were defending them on foreign soil.

Higher wages produced increased income tax revenue for the United States, providing the government more capital to loan to the Allied nations in Europe. In a relatively short time, the United States went from being chronically in debt to foreign governments, which it had been since its founding in 1776, to loaning large sums of money to other nations. During and after the war, the United States loaned $11 billion to the Allied nations. When the conflict ended on November 11, 1918, the country returned to a peacetime economy, but this proved harder than anyone imagined.

Coming Home

When World War I ended, American soldiers expected to reap the benefits of the productivity and prosperity the war had brought to the United States. But the sudden decrease in demand for exported food and wartime goods brought on by the war's end did not result in a corresponding reduction in production levels. Farmers and factories continued to produce at wartime levels, flooding the market to the point that prices dropped and surpluses accumulated. Not enough people at home were buying what was being produced, and the European Allies were too preoccupied with putting their own nations and lives back together to provide new markets for the glut of products.

American businessmen and farmers should have been concerned about this trade imbalance, but no one seemed to notice—or care. Americans' joy over the end of the war took the form of continuous celebration. The stock market rose steadily, the economy seemed to be on a strong footing, and women achieved a long-time dream of gaining the right to vote. Euphoria spawned a rampant materialism that changed the way Americans spent money. According to historian and author Robert S. McElvaine, "These were the days when America withdrew from the world and went into an orgy of self-indulgence."[8] One group that some historians have singled out as the epitome of this spirit of self-indulgence was young American women.

Women's Rights

The Nineteenth Amendment to the Constitution, granting women voting rights, was proposed on June 4, 1919, and eventually ratified by the states. Although few women of that time showed much interest in politics, they demonstrated a passion for finally being considered equal to men. In Addition this new political equality, women also sought social

Women work with pneumatic hammers in a military ordnance factory in Pennsylvania in 1918. The US enjoyed a robust economy during World War I and, with the nation's men going to war, women played a large part in that economy.

equality. They cut their hair short, and their skirt lengths rose. Young women danced with abandon and many smoked. They also learned to drive the country's newest mechanical contraption—the Model T Ford, lovingly referred to by many as the Tin Lizzie. They were known as *flappers*—a term widely linked at the time to the fashion of wearing galoshes unbuckled so that they flapped as the wearer walked.

Historian and author Ernest R. May describes the young women of post–World War I America—whom he calls "the daughters of the American middle class"—as "the shock troops of the 'antipuritan revolt.'"[9] In order to have more leisure time, women wanted to be free of the drudgery of housework. They wanted all the newfangled contraptions that were flooding the market, such as washing machines and vacuum cleaners, and they wanted phonographs and telephones and other conveniences. Up until the 1920s the practice among most American families had been to save up for any necessities or luxuries until they could be paid for in full. But the country overflowed with new inventions that most were no longer willing to wait for.

Buying on Credit

To answer this demand, a novel method of purchasing goods was born, while, at the same time, the age-old goal of saving for a rainy day was discouraged. McElvaine explains:

> Old habits of thrift and sacrifice, deeply ingrained in early stages of industrialism, now were to be altered, if not reversed, and advertisers would be the instructors in the new ways. All the virtues of the age of scarcity were now questioned. . . . Advertisers spread this new consumer ethic widely in the prosperity decade: Don't tighten your belts, loosen them—the more we spend the more prosperous we'll be.[10]

Buying on credit was the brainchild of advertising men such as Edward Bernays, an advertising executive whose ad campaign encouraged women to smoke Lucky Strike cigarettes, and Albert D. Lasker, who advertised Kleenex, Palmolive soap, Pepsodent toothpaste, and Sunkist oranges. Ad campaigns run by these men and many others engendered an enormous desire among American middle-class women to own things immediately that they had previously waited years to buy.

However, with wages climbing more slowly than production levels, it seemed impossible for the average family to afford all the conveniences they wanted, even at bargain prices. To rectify this situation, advertising agencies came up with a way to get Americans to buy more with less money—buying credit with the help of an installment plan. For a small down payment and easy monthly or weekly payments—plus interest—families could own a washing machine and other appliances without having to wait until they had the cash to cover the full amount. Helping to fuel this materialism across the nation was another new product that virtually every household in America desired—the radio.

Prohibition

The Eighteenth Amendment to the US Constitution, ratified January 16, 1919, took effect on January 17, 1920. It banned the sale, manufacture, and transportation of alcohol, but it was not illegal for Americans to possess or consume alcohol.

Opponents of Prohibition were called *Wets*. Proponents were called *Dries*. Wets called the ban an assault on the rights of everyday life in the United States. Alcohol was stockpiled widely in 1919 before the amendment took effect. Prohibition was intended to reduce crime, but the opposite proved true. Gangsters such as the notorious Al Capone produced alcohol or smuggled it into the country and sold it, a practice known as bootlegging.

Prohibition was widely supported by Dries, mostly women, religious leaders, and church members, as a means of societal improvement. Texas senator Morris Sheppard quipped in 1930 that "there is as much chance of repealing the 18th Amendment as there is for a hummingbird to fly to the planet Mars with the Washington Monument tied to its tail." He was wrong.

On February 20, 1933, another amendment to the Constitution was proposed that abolished Prohibition. President Roosevelt signed the Cullen-Harrison Act on March 22, 1933, legalizing the sale of wine and weak beer. The Twenty-First Amendment was ratified on December 5, 1933. It is the only amendment in the US Constitution that repeals a previous amendment.

Charles Merz, *The Dry Decade*. Seattle: University of Washington Press, 1969, p. *ix*.

Radio

Radio had its beginnings almost simultaneously in Europe and America in the last years of the nineteenth century. In the United States, Nikola Tesla, and in Italy, Guglielmo Marconi, both perfected wireless telegraphy or wireless telephony—sending Morse code signals through the air. A few years later, it was discovered that other sounds—for example, music and the human voice—could also be broadcast over large distances.

It was not until November 2, 1920, however, that the first commercial radio broadcast was made in the United States. That broadcast from station KDKA in Pittsburgh, Pennsylvania, aired election results of the Harding-Cox presidential race. Soon other stations began airing music, news, sporting events, live concerts, church services, and other public events. According to journalist Fredrick Lewis Allen in *Only Yesterday: An Informal History of the 1920's*: "When the Unknown Soldier was buried at Arlington Cemetery [in 1921] . . . crowds packed into Madison Square Garden in New York and the Auditorium in San Francisco to hear the speeches issue from huge amplifiers, and few in those crowds had any idea that soon they could hear all the orations they wanted without stirring from the easy-chair in the livingroom."[11]

Back in 1916 David Sarnoff, a pioneer in the radio and television broadcasting industries, had approached Edward J. Nally, head of the Marconi Company in America, with the idea of designing a "Radio Music Box" for every household in the country, to play music, pass along news, and provide entertainment. This suggestion led to the formation of RCA—the Radio Corporation of America. In 1922 retail sales of RCA radios reached $11 million. Two years later, annual sales totaled $60 million. By the end of the decade, RCA radio sales had reached $842.5 million.

Seventy-six commercial radio stations were on the air in July 1922. By the end of that year the number had increased to five hundred stations, spanning the country. Americans were hooked. By the early 1930s they could follow what was happening around the country and be entertained by radio programs such as *Amos and Andy*, *Jack Benny*, and *The Lone Ranger*. When the Great Depression hit at the end of the 1920s, radio provided a lifeline of hope to people drowning in despair, but during the early and mid-1920s, radio mirrored the optimism, prosperity, and celebration of life in post–World War I America.

American women enjoyed many new freedoms in the years before the Great Depression. Fashions of the 1920s (pictured) are but one example of the changes enjoyed by women.

Coolidge Prosperity

During the presidential campaign of 1920, Republican candidate War-ren G. Harding called for a return to "normalcy." This desire to return to prewar life—an "America first" attitude insulating the United States from foreign entanglements and influences—struck a chord with the nation, resulting in his election. Harding and his vice president, Calvin Coolidge, assumed office on March 4, 1921, riding a wave of optimism and prosperity they felt would last for decades to come. But Harding died suddenly in San Francisco, California, on August 2, 1923, thrusting Coolidge into the presidency. An era known as Coolidge Prosperity began in late 1923.

Coolidge completed Harding's term and was elected in 1924. "Silent Cal," as he became known, earned his nickname by doing and saying very little during his term of office. Coolidge felt that the less the federal government interfered in people's lives, the better. He also supported the growth of big business—in effect helping the richest people in the country become even richer. He summed up his economic philosophy in a speech given before the American Society of Newspaper Editors in Washington, DC, on January 17, 1925: "The chief business of the American people is business." He later wrote, "The man who builds a factory builds a temple. The man who works there worships there."[12]

According to McElvaine, Coolidge's devotion to business and to governmental nonaction was a major factor contributing to the Great Depression:

> His [Coolidge's] refusal to worry about the problems of the future, along with his complete deference to business, was perceived by people with the benefit of hindsight as causes of the economic collapse. "If you see ten troubles coming down the road, Coolidge had said, "you can be sure that nine will run into the ditch before they reach you." This attitude epitomized the twenties; the consequences it helped to produce were grim.[13]

During the 1920s, with huge tax breaks being given to the rich and much smaller breaks passed along to the poor, the gap between the ultrarich and those living in poverty widened into what became known among economists and sociologists as the maldistribution of wealth. The income of the twenty-four thousand richest families in the country—0.1 percent of the population—equaled that of the bottom 42 percent of the population—11.5 million people. The nation's wealth was controlled by only a small percentage of the population, and the gap between rich and poor widened every day, thanks to those with money investing more and more in the booming stock market.

Buying on Margin

Just as purchasing household goods with only a small down payment became popular in the 1920s, so too did buying shares of stock in the same way. In order to buy more stocks and make a profit by selling those stocks when they increased in value, the practice of installment buying expanded to buying stock on speculation. This meant the buyer paid only 10 percent of the cost of the stock and borrowed the other 90 percent from the stockbroker, using the shares as collateral for the loan. When the stock price rose, the buyer sold the stock, repaid the loan from the broker, and reaped a nice profit. This practice was called buying on margin. According to American economist John Kenneth Galbraith, Americans were "displaying an inordinate desire to get rich quickly with a minimum of physical effort. . . . Men and women [were building] a world of speculative make-believe. This is a world inhabited not by people who have to be persuaded to believe but by people who want an excuse to believe."[14]

Wherever people looked, they were being encouraged to not only spend the money they were earning but to also borrow money to spend on things they wanted and could not afford without buying on the installment plan. More and more, people who were far from rich decided to invest in the stock market. Americans quickly went deeply into debt, investors got rich speculating on stocks, and almost everyone felt Coolidge Prosperity would last forever. According to McElvaine:

The idea that a penny saved is a penny earned was passé. It was now to be: Spend the penny before you earn it. It was no longer necessary to save for a rainy day, since in the New Era of eternal prosperity the sun would always shine.

By the last years of the decade, three of every five cars and 80 percent of all radios were purchased with installment credit. Between 1925 and 1929 the amount of installment credit outstanding in the United States more than doubled, from $1.38 billion to $3 billion.[15]

The Ballyhoo Years

The 1920s, because of their rowdy, uninhibited nature, have been called the Ballyhoo Years, the Roaring Twenties, the Jazz Age, the Prosperity

Car Crazy

In the first decades of the twentieth century the United States was on the move, and nothing illustrated that better than the explosive growth of the automobile industry. In 1919 cars were fairly rare, with Henry Ford's black Model T the most popular model. During the 1920s the Model T was replaced with other makes, models, and colors of automobiles. In 1919, 90 per cent of all cars were open in design. By 1929, 90 percent were enclosed. The number of vehicles on the road increased from fewer than 7 million in 1919 to 27 million by 1929.

By 1925, cars were being produced on assembly lines at the rate of one every ten seconds. This resulted in lower prices, making cars more affordable to Americans. Before World War I, a car would have cost the buyer two years' earnings, but by 1929 a car cost only three months' earnings. No matter the cost, though, the car gave freedom to those who were looking for ways to escape their everyday lives. And no longer did the buyer have to pay the full purchase price for a new car, since the creation of the installment plan. By 1926 the vast majority of buyers were buying cars on credit.

Decade, the Era of Excess, and the Era of Wonderful Nonsense. It was a seemingly carefree time but also a time of contrasts. According to McElvaine, "It was a time of political conservatism and moral latitude, of great prosperity and grinding poverty . . . a time in which the American people, and particularly their leaders, were treading water when they should have been swimming vigorously."[16] The booming stock market—called a bull market—seemed to know no boundaries. The more people bought stock on margin, the higher the market climbed. Financial experts knew the boom could not last forever, but no one seemed inclined to listen to the few who warned about the inevitable crash.

The market suffered an abrupt drop in value—sometimes called a hiccup—in June of 1928, and losses wiped away earlier gains. On June 12 the market set a record of more than 5 million shares traded, more than a million above the all-time high of almost 3.9 million set in March 1928. To make matters worse, the ticker—the machine displaying stock trades—fell almost two hours behind, leaving investors clueless about the value of their stocks. Many thought the bull market had collapsed, but the momentary slump passed, and the boom continued.

The Climb Before the Fall

Nineteen twenty-eight brought an enormous increase in margin buying that the slump in June could not stop. Americans were in a frenzy to participate in the get-rich-quick aspects of the market. Anyone could turn a small investment into a small fortune in a short time. According to Watkins:

> The "Great Bull Market" expanded like a flowering nova in 1928 and 1929, driven by a kind of mass madness. . . . In 1927, there had been 577 million shares traded on the New York Stock Exchange; in 1928, the figure was 920 million. The pace accelerated during the first nine months of 1929; indeed, between August and September transactions on the floor of the New York Exchange were already speeding toward the 1.1 billion shares that would end the year.[17]

The stock market was not the only lure for individuals and companies seeking profits. By the end of 1928, margin loans were returning an incredible 12 percent, meaning a person could buy stock for $100 and soon afterward sell the same stock for $112. American corporations realized they could put their capital to better use investing in stock rather than using that money to produce goods in an already glutted market. According to Galbraith, "A great river of gold began to converge on Wall Street," but the good fortune and exhilaration of the moment were fleeting. The year 1928 was the last year for a long time that Americans were "buoyant, uninhibited, and utterly happy. It wasn't that 1928 was too good to last; it was only that it didn't last."[18]

Chapter 2

Ignoring the Signs

Various historians and economists have tried to describe what happened in the United States during 1929 that led to the Great Depression, but their descriptions are often too complex to be readily understood. Two analogies, though, are worthy of mention. They provide relatively clear descriptions of the behaviors and practices that caused the economic collapse that began mid-year and culminated in the stock market crash of October 29.

John Kenneth Galbraith compares the fragile state of the 1929 American economy to a bubble about to burst. Early in the year, he says, economists had hoped for a gradual end to the speculation boom, but fears of a catastrophic economic crash overshadowed that optimism. According to Galbraith, "A bubble can easily be punctured. But to incise it with a needle so that it subsides gradually is a task of no small delicacy. Among those who sensed what was happening in early 1929, there was some hope but no confidence that the boom could be made to subside. The real choice was between an immediate and deliberately engineered collapse and a more serious disaster later on."[19]

Robert S. McElvaine, on the other hand, compares the nation's risky 1929 investment behavior to a person who drinks too much alcohol and then gets behind the wheel of a car: "Stock speculation provided a legal spirit of intoxication in a time when intoxicating spirits were prohibited by the Eighteenth Amendment. By the fall of 1929, those who were guiding the market were driving under the influence. A terrible crash, to be followed by unpleasant sobering experiences and an awful hangover were the likely results."[20]

Both analogies, as it turns out, are accurate.

Ignoring the Warning Signs

Early in 1929 stock market speculation was at an all-time high. The country was also in the midst of a change in the Oval Office. After Coolidge announced he would not seek a second full term, Republican Herbert Hoover was elected in November 1928. In his acceptance speech, he confidently proclaimed: "We in America today are nearer to the final triumph over poverty than ever before in the history of any land. The poorhouse is vanishing from among us. We have not yet reached the goal, but, given a chance to go forward with the policies of the last eight years, we shall soon, with the help of God, be in sight of the day when poverty will be banished from this nation."[21]

As Hoover's March 4 inauguration approached, confidence among investors soared. The Great Bull Market continued booming. According to Galbraith, despite warning signs, outgoing President Coolidge "neither knew nor cared what was going on. A few days before leaving office in 1929, he cheerily observed that things were 'absolutely sound' and that stocks were 'cheap at current prices.' In earlier years, whenever warned that speculation was getting out of hand, he had comforted himself with the thought that this was the primary responsibility of the Federal Reserve Board."[22]

The Federal Reserve Board of Governors was the agency responsible for guiding and directing the nation's central banking system—the twelve Federal Reserve banks. In actuality, board members had little power and virtually no incentive to intervene. If they took action to stop the boom, and it backfired, plunging the country instead into economic turmoil, they feared being blamed.

The board was slow to do anything that might bring an end to investors' prosperity. Instead of taking decisive action, such as issuing a stern warning to investors, it decided to proceed cautiously. It issued two lengthy letters—on February 2 and on February 7—to New York banks, urging caution in financing margin buying in the market. It did not, however, recommend immediate action. The result of this overly cautious step was a slight dip in the market on February 7, but it did not last. Buying resumed at previous levels, then increased.

The Pecora Hearings

In January 1933 the Senate Banking and Currency Committee met under the counsel of a former district attorney from New York City, Ferdinand Pecora. Pecora was seeking to learn the causes of the Great Depression. During the hearings he questioned bankers to determine whether any of their actions had contributed to the stock market crash.

The bankers questioned by the committee included Charles E. Mitchell of National City Bank and Albert H. Wiggin of Chase Bank. Wiggin admitted that he had reduced the price of Chase shares and made substantial profits as a result. Mitchell and other officers of National City had given themselves interest-free loans totaling $2.4 million when they saw the crash coming. They also shifted bad loans by selling securities to investors in Latin American countries, who had no idea disaster was imminent.

Next, Pecora zeroed in on J.P. Morgan Bank. Morgan partners reluctantly admitted that despite their vast fortunes, they had paid no income taxes for 1931 or 1932 after suffering losses in the crash. Pecora also extracted the shocking news that Morgan's preferred list for discounted stock offerings included former president Coolidge and Supreme Court justice Owen J. Roberts.

The Pecora Hearings laid the foundation for financial reform legislation for the banking system. The Securities Act of 1933, the Glass-Stegall Act of 1933, and the Securities Exchange Act of 1934 all addressed issues raised by the hearings. Pecora was subsequently named a commissioner of the newly formed Securities and Exchange Commission (SEC).

Government Inaction

When Hoover took office, optimism among Americans remained high, and the market continued booming. Toward the end of March, the Federal Reserve board members met daily but remained silent about what they discussed. Their silence made the country nervous. When they held their first-ever Saturday meeting, yet still maintained silence, the country's investors reacted with apprehension.

The following week, investors began selling stocks, banks held back on loans, and stockbrokers raised interest rates on margin buying to 14 percent. Across the board, prices fell precipitously. It looked as though the Great Bull Market might have reached its end. However, investment banker Charles E. Mitchell, chairman of the board of National City Bank (now Citibank), made the following announcement to the press: "We feel that we have an obligation which is paramount to any Federal Reserve warning, or anything else, to avert any dangerous crisis in the money market."[23] He promised that National City would loan as much money as necessary to prevent the end of the investment boom. His words worked magic.

By the end of the day, the market stabilized. The Federal Reserve remained silent and took no action, but now its silence was interpreted by private investors as a good thing. In truth, the market—because of the Federal Reserve's inaction at this point—was virtually assured of not being subject to governmental interference. The effect was similar to what happens when a red flag is waved in the face of a charging bull: The waving flag makes the charge more intense—and more dangerous. In the case of the market, the boom continued.

Had Mitchell and his bank not taken action, the bull market might have ended in March 1929. Prices might have continued falling, and the nation might have suffered a moderate to severe depression. Thus, if any one man can be credited—or blamed—for putting off that financial inevitability until its fall brought about the Great Depression, that man would be Mitchell.

Investment Trusts

The steps Mitchell took in March may have delayed the inevitable financial collapse some feared lay ahead, but, in truth, it was the reckless investing practices that people like Mitchell had encouraged through-out the 1920s that made the crash catastrophic when it occurred in the fall of 1929. Speculation allowed people with little money to buy stocks in companies they knew little about, but at least those shares represent-ed partial ownership in companies that produced goods or provided services. Another type of investment, called investment trusts, neither produced goods nor provided services.

An investment trust was a collection of stocks from various com-panies, grouped into one entity. Investors could buy into these trusts, which used the capital to buy shares in another, usually larger trust. The sequence continued, until vast amounts of investment capital were tied up in what were hundreds of giant pyramid schemes. According to T.H. Watkins, these trusts were "building nothing, manufacturing nothing, selling nothing but paper shares in their paper selves."[24] Journalist Steve Wiegand adds, "Instead of money going into businesses so that they could expand, make new products, and hire more people, much of that money just floated between trusts for speculation schemes."[25]

The buying frenzy continued through mid-1929 in stocks and trusts, with most investors becoming drunk on profits and oblivious to the instability of the market. Financial advisers contributed to the fren-zy, urging people to buy, buy, buy, while prices soared. In August 1929 an article written by John J. Raskob, a Wall Street mogul, appeared in *Ladies' Home Journal*. Raskob's article, titled "Everybody Ought to Be Rich," urged people to invest $15 monthly in the stock market and not to spend any dividends. This would, he predicted, earn the investor $80,000 within ten years. Even as the article was being read, however, Raskob was quietly selling his own stocks.

The Babson Break

Many historians say the crash the stock market experienced on Octo-ber 29, 1929, actually began a month and a half earlier, on Labor Day. The Dow Jones Industrial Average, a closely watched statistical average of thirty large, publicly owned US companies, increased in value by more than 25 percent during June, July, and August. Trading volume was heavy, frequently between 4 million and 5 million shares a day.

More than a month before the October 1929 stock market crash,
investment adviser Roger W. Babson (pictured) predicted a
devastating financial crash that would lead to a depression. Many
Wall Street financial analysts of the time criticized the gloomy
predictions made by Babson and others.

Brokers' loans increased during the summer at the rate of $400 mil-
lion a month as people stampeded the market to buy stocks on margin. The lure of quick fortunes was so overwhelming that anyone who
dared predict anything other than continued prosperity and growth
was soundly criticized.

Some investment advisers did urge caution, however. Roger W.
Babson, at his annual National Business Conference, on September 5
predicted, "Sooner or later a crash is coming, and it may be terrific."
He also predicted a drop of sixty to eighty points in the Dow Jones
averages, that "factories will shut down," that "men will be thrown out
of work," and that "the result will be a serious business depression."[26]

Babson was far from alone in his dire predictions, but Wall Street's inner circle criticized these naysayers for their gloomy outlook. They conceded that a recession might occur when the boom finally burst, but that it would not be severe. The Babson Break, as the market downturn was named, came Thursday, September 5. From that point, the market dropped, then rallied a bit, then dropped again. The overall trend was downward. Wall Street moguls called it a technical adjustment.

Additional investment trusts continued to be launched, speculators were still eager to invest, and brokers' loans continued to rise. Galbraith sums it up: "By the autumn of 1929 the economy was well into a depression. In June the indexes of industrial and of factory production both reached a peak and turned down. By October, the Federal Reserve index of industrial production stood at 117 as compared with 126 four months earlier. . . . Finally, down came the stock market."[27]

The Downward Slide

Important people on Wall Street seemed to be frantically participating in the age-old tradition of incantation. They seemed to believe that if they stated the economy was sound often enough, it would remain sound. By announcing that prosperity would continue, they hoped prosperity would indeed continue. However, nothing could stop the steady decline of the economy and, along with it, the stock market. When people who had invested in the market lost their confidence in making money, they backed away, selling instead of buying. The result was a massive readjustment that turned into panic.

Those who refused to accept the downward slide continued, until October 24, offering investors what turned out to be false hope. The Harvard Economic Society, for example, indicated that it did not believe the slump in stock prices was "the precursor of a business depression."[28] Colonel Leonard P. Ayres of the Cleveland Trust Company said on October 15, "There does not seem to be as yet much real evidence that the decline in stock prices is likely to forecast a serious recession in general business."[29]

In early October Mitchell again attempted to bolster investor confidence when he made the following announcements: "The industrial situation of the United States is absolutely sound and our credit situation is in no way critical. . . . The markets generally are now in a healthy condition. . . . The market values have a sound basis in the general prosperity of our country."[30] Investors, however, refused to listen. The market continued its slide.

Black Thursday

On Monday, October 21, the market ticker once again fell behind in reporting the trading volume. Investors had no way of knowing what was happening to their stocks. They could be ruined financially and not be aware of it for hours. Toward the end of trading, though, the market rallied, and final quotes were higher than previous lows for the day's trading. The day's final transaction, however, was not reported until an hour and forty minutes after the market closed, leaving investors uninformed as to the status of their stock portfolios until it was too late to do anything about it. On Wednesday the market demonstrated further losses, and the ticker again fell behind. Investors were selling in a fearful frenzy.

On Thursday, October 24, nearly 13 million shares changed hands, mostly at rock-bottom prices, wiping out fortunes stockholders had made in previous months. For every sale, though, there must be a buyer. On Black Thursday, as this day came to be called, offers to sell were not always met with offers to buy. By 11:00 a.m. brokers were frantically trying to sell at any price. According to Galbraith, "By eleven thirty the market had surrendered to blind, relentless fear. This, indeed, was panic."[31]

But the panic ended after the chaotic morning, thanks to a group of New York bankers. After a meeting at the offices of J.P. Morgan and Company, they strode through the crowds that had gathered in the streets. Mitchell of National City Bank, Albert H. Wiggin of Chase National Bank, William C. Potter of the Guaranty Trust Company, Seward Prosser of the Bankers Trust Company, and Thomas W. Lamont of J.P. Morgan entered the stock exchange. Having agreed to provide organized support for the market, they wandered through the exchange,

From Hero to Villain

Charles E. Mitchell was an American banker and chairman of National City Bank during the Great Depression. Through announcements that the market was sound and there was nothing to worry about, Mitchell helped bolster the stock market during the months leading up to the crash. After he and other bankers entered the stock exchange on Black Thursday, October 24, 1929, and purchased stock in order to restore investor confidence and prevent collapse, he was hailed as a hero.

However, Mitchell was later vilified as having conducted unethical business that contributed in part to the economic collapse. Millions of shares of bank stock were sold, netting the bank $650 million, but most of this was lost when the stock market crashed on October 29, 1929. He sold National City stock to his wife for a substantial loss, just so he could avoid paying income taxes in 1929. Later, Mitchell purchased the stock back from his wife at the same low price he had sold it to her for—all without her knowledge. Though legal at the time, his actions were considered unethical.

Mitchell was indicted for tax evasion after the hearings, but he was found not guilty of the criminal charges filed against him. However, the government filed a $1.1 million civil claim against him for unpaid taxes and penalties, and won. Mitchell appealed the verdict to the Supreme Court, and lost. He eventually settled the claim, but not until December 17, 1938.

buying stock in large quantities. Fear and panic vanished. The bankers acted decisively, and the frenzy of selling ended. The market's recovery in the afternoon equaled the panic of the morning. The market was saved—for the moment.

Mixed Emotions

Even with the bankers' support of the market, thousands of investors lost everything in the panic. It was 7:08 p.m. before everyone knew the bottom line of the day's trading and the extent of the devastating losses. Mitchell and others continued to spout assurances that the market was fundamentally sound. On Friday and Saturday, the market continued experiencing heavy trading, but prices were, for the most part, steady. The panic subsided, and there was a general feeling of optimism that the worst was over. The single criticism, ignored in the wake of the seeming recovery, came from then–New York governor Franklin Delano Roosevelt, who blamed the panic on the "fever of speculation."[32]

Investor optimism did not last. When the stock exchange opened on Monday, October 28, the order of the day was to sell, not to buy. Nine and a quarter million shares changed hands, resulting in even more devastation than on Black Thursday. The ticker fell behind. This time the market made no miraculous recovery. During the last hour, more than 3 million shares traded, each with a price less than the one before. Bankers once again met, but this time, to everyone's horror, they issued a statement that they would not maintain stock prices or protect investors' profits. Instead they announced that they hoped to see the market remain orderly on its own. That Monday evening the country again held its breath. The worst was yet to come.

Black Tuesday

Tuesday, October 29, 1929, was the most disastrous day in the history of the New York Stock Exchange. As bad as the days leading up to it had been, Black Tuesday was far worse. The minute the market opened, orders to sell poured in. Investors took what they could get, but there were not enough buyers to match offers to sell. The ticker was a staggering two and a half hours behind at the close of trading. Nearly 16.5 million transactions were recorded, with many others undoubtedly undocumented. The Dow Industrial Average fell forty-three points, wiping out all gains realized over the preceding year. The biggest losers of the day were the investment trusts. They fell to practically nothing.

At last, the horrible day ended. Stock exchange employees worked through the night to record the transactions. Over the previous week, amateur speculators had been wiped out, followed by professional investors, the well-to-do, and then the wealthy. Those who saw the crash coming and liquidated their holdings early retained most of their investments. Those who stayed to ride out the end of the Great Bull Market suffered terrible losses. Bankers, hailed as heroes on Black Thursday, were reviled for their abandonment of support on Black Tuesday.

Panicked stock traders crowd sidewalks outside of the New York Stock Exchange on October 29, 1929—the day of the historic stock market crash. By day's end, the downward slide of the Dow Industrial Average had wiped out all financial gains of the preceding year.

Amazingly, the market experienced moderate gains on October 30 and 31. Trading was fairly even until the market suffered another slump on Monday, November 5. November 11–13 are thought by some to have been the worst days of the crash. During these three days the Dow Industrials lost another fifty points, down a total of eighty-two points since Labor Day.

There were no further attempts at organized support to bolster the market. Some investors and brokers committed suicide because of the crash, but the myth of hundreds of such suicides is just that—a myth. The suicide rate did not rise substantially above normal during the last months of 1929. However, the nation's suicide rate did increase over the next three years, as the country sank deeper into the Great Depression.

President Herbert Hoover

President Hoover seemed indifferent to the fate of the stock market but paid attention to the corresponding decline in the price of commodities. Commodities are goods and services whose prices are based on global supply and demand, as in the case of copper, wheat, or oil. Hoover also paid attention to the decline in production levels—how much of each that was produced, manufactured, or grown—of commodities such as iron, steel, wheat, and coal, as well as the production level of automobiles.

Americans stopped their excessive buying and held onto the money they still had, fearing what the future might bring. Even radio sales dropped to half the previous level. To try to boost spending among consumers, Hoover cut taxes by one percentage point for all Americans. For the poorest of the population, this resulted in a tax cut of less than four dollars, while the wealthiest Americans enjoyed substantial tax reductions. This did not produce the boost to the economy Hoover hoped to achieve. The wealthy held onto their money instead of spending it to stimulate the economy. The market exhibited sizable recoveries in January, February, and March of 1930, but in April it dropped again, and continued to drop every week for two more years.

The Dow Industrials closed on November 13, 1929, at 224. By July 8, 1932, they were at 58. During these three years of decline, the country sank into the worst economic depression ever suffered. Throughout this time, Hoover continued to assure the American people that business would rebound and that everything would be back to normal within the next few months. He maintained that it was not the role of the federal government to interfere in the daily lives of Americans. He left relief efforts up to families, religious organizations, communities, cities, and states. Resources were quickly drained, however, and the recovery Hoover kept promising was smothered beneath an avalanche of unemployment, hunger, and despair.

Chapter 3

From Bad to Worse

During the Great Depression, two presidents led the nation—Herbert Hoover and Franklin Delano Roosevelt. They came from different political parties, had opposite political and economic philosophies, and approached the problems of the nation in completely different ways. One has been vilified by many for helping cause the Depression—or at least for not doing anything decisive to remedy it—and the other lavishly praised by many for his role in bringing the nation out of the Depression. Neither assessment is without exaggeration; characterizations vary from one historian to the next. Yet all who have studied the Great Depression agree on this central point: Conditions for average Americans were extremely difficult during the Great Depression.

Hoover's Response

Between October 1929 and November 1932, Hoover did little to improve worsening economic conditions. He felt the economy was adjusting after a period of uncontrolled growth and that it would recover. For months after the crash, Hoover refused to believe unemployed people in the United States might not be able to feed their families and that some were actually starving.

In mid-1932, toward the end of his term, Hoover told reporters the conditions of the poor in America were exaggerated. He said, "Nobody is actually starving. The hobos are actually better fed than they have ever been. One hobo in New York got ten meals in one day."[33] But people *were* starving, many suffering from diseases related to malnutrition, such as pellagra and rickets. Patrick Jay Hurley, secretary of war during the Hoover administration, stated the philosophy of that administration: "To give a gratuity to an individual is divesting men and women of their spirit, their self-reliance. It is striking at the very foundation of the system on which the nation is built."[34] According to Steve Wiegand, Hurley, like many in Washington at the time, "seemed to consider poverty a moral defect."[35]

In late 1929 Hoover called business leaders to the White House for a series of conferences. The purpose of these meetings, it seemed, was not to formulate strategies to help Americans. Instead, they seemed to have been called so Hoover could encourage those assembled to exhibit confidence in the economy by investing in their own companies and in others. He apparently hoped this would be sufficient to turn the economy around.

The market enjoyed a bit of revival through the end of 1929 and into the spring of 1930, but hope created by this temporary upswing proved false. A closer look revealed that sales and production were down, people were being laid off in mass numbers, profits were declining, and no matter how desperately people tried to smile and hope for the best, every day brought worse news.

Clearly, the economy was in trouble, and no amount of expressed optimism on the part of Hoover or business leaders could change the downward spiral that sucked the nation into ever-deepening depression. American historian H. Paul Jeffers summarizes the disturbing economic statistics and explains Hoover's response to the nation's situation:

> Since the peak of Coolidge Prosperity, the Gross National Product had gone down by 29 percent. Consumer buying dipped 18 percent. Construction was off by 78 percent. Investment plummeted 98 percent. The rate of unemployment zoomed from 3.2 percent to nearly one fourth of the working population. . . . Early in 1931 President Hoover said, "What this country needs is a good big laugh." The way to dispel "a condition of hysteria," he ventured, "was for someone to get off a good joke every ten days."[36]

It became disturbingly clear from Hoover's inaction, and responses such as these, that he had no idea what to do.

Unemployment During the Great Depression

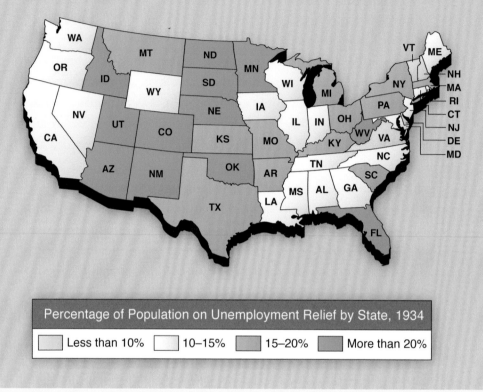

Percentage of Population on Unemployment Relief by State, 1934

Less than 10%   10–15%   15–20%   More than 20%

No Jobs, No Money, No Hope

Millions of Americans lost their jobs between 1929 and 1932 because employers could no longer pay their wages. Those who managed to retain their jobs took home only a fraction of the money they had earned before as production, wages, and work hours were cut. By the end of 1931 hundreds of thousands of Americans could no longer afford to pay rent or make house payments. With few options, they either lived on the streets or in temporary shelters. In Philadelphia, for example, as many as thirteen hundred evictions a month are estimated to have taken place. Scholars believe that by the end of 1933 nearly half of all home mortgages were in default. People who lost their homes sometimes stayed with family, at least for a while, squatted in abandoned buildings with neither running water nor electricity, or took to the road, desperately seeking work.

When no work could be found, people often ended up living in shacks, sheds, or tents in thrown-together communities on the outskirts of cities. Every city of any size had such a community, usually on vacant land on the edge of town or in industrial districts. They quickly became known as Hoovervilles, named for the person many blamed for allowing the Depression to happen—President Hoover. The Oakland, California, Hooverville was a field of abandoned concrete sewer pipes. In San Francisco, it was made up of old trolley cars. St. Louis had one of the nation's largest Hoovervilles, with separate, distinct neighborhoods.

Each of these temporary communities was unique, but they shared some common characteristics. Most were located near charities that gave out food or secondhand clothing. All were illegal and their residents considered trespassers, but cities usually tolerated them because they did not know what else to do with their homeless. Most cities required their Hooverville residents to abide by minimal health and safety regulations such as proper disposal of trash and sewage, keeping cooking fires in appropriate receptacles, and boiling drinking water. Some Hoovervilles had their own governments, adopted rules and regulations, and even occasionally saw shanties within their communities bought and sold.

T.H. Watkins describes the living conditions of a typical Depression-era homeless person:

Those homeless who did not drift—and there were thousands in every city of any size at all—slept in lice-ridden and rat-infested flophouses when they could afford the ten or fifteen cents for a urine-soaked mattress on the floor, and on park benches, under park shrubbery and bridge abutments, in doorways, packing crates, concrete pipes, culverts, construction sites, and abandoned automobiles when they could not afford it. The more ambitious among them contrived fragile shelters from scraps of wood and cardboard, old beer signs and fence posts, anything they could find that would keep off the wind and rain of winter and the direct sun of summer.[37]

E.J. Sullivan, who experienced the Depression, transformed Psalm 23 into a parody called "The 1932nd Psalm" to express his opinion of Hoover. It was an opinion shared by millions of lower- and middle-class Americans; it reads:

Hoover is my Shepherd, I am in want,
He maketh me to lie down on park benches,
He leadeth me by still factories,
He restoreth my doubt in the Republican Party.
He guided me in the path of the Unemployed for his party's sake,
Yea, though I walk through the alley of soup kitchens,
I am hungry.
I do not fear evil, for thou art against me;
Thy Cabinet and thy Senate, they do discomfort me;
Thou didst prepare a reduction in my wages;
In the presence of my creditors thou anointed my income with taxes,
So my expenses overrunneth my income.
Surely, poverty and hard times will follow me
All the days of the Republican administration,
And I shall dwell in a rented house forever.
Amen.[38]

As the presidential election of 1932 approached, Americans turned to someone else for answers to what could be done to salvage the economy and pull the nation out of the Depression.

Roosevelt's Election

As governor of New York, Franklin Roosevelt had faced economic challenges. He had warned of the coming national catastrophe, but no one had listened. In 1932 he gained the Democratic Party's nomination for president. Breaking the tradition that a party's candidate should not appear at his party's convention after being selected, Roosevelt flew to Chicago and addressed the crowd. The end of his acceptance speech became the theme for his administration's efforts to heal the nation: "I pledge

Roosevelt's Inaugural Address

On March 4, 1933, Roosevelt was inaugurated as the thirty-second president of the United States. In his speech he outlined immense challenges facing the nation's citizens but also offered hope for the future:

> The withered leaves of industrial enterprise lie on every side; farmers find no markets for their produce; the savings of many years in thousands of families is gone. More important, a host of unemployed citizens face the grim problem of existence, and an equally great number toil with little return. Only a foolish optimist can deny the dark realities of the moment.
>
> Yet our distress comes from no failure of substance. We are stricken by no plague of locusts. Compared with the perils which our forefathers conquered because they believed and were not afraid, we have still much to be thankful for. Nature still offers her bounty, and human efforts have multiplied it. Plenty is at our doorstep, but a generous use of it languishes in the very sight of the supply.
>
> Happiness lies not in the mere possession of money. It lies in the joy of achievement, in the thrill of creative effort. The joy and moral stimulation of work no longer must be forgotten in the mad chase of evanescent profits. These dark days will be worth all they cost if they teach us that our true destiny is not to be ministered unto but to minister to ourselves and to our fellow men.

Quoted in Robert Torricelli and Andrew Carroll, eds., *In Our Own Words: Extraordinary Speeches of the American Century.* New York: Kodansha International, 1999, pp. 100–101.

you, I pledge myself, to a new deal for the American people."[39] From that point on, Roosevelt's programs were called the New Deal.

After defeating Hoover in November 1932, Roosevelt immediately gathered men he knew could help shape the nation's recovery. The challenges the president and his advisers faced, according to author William E. Leuchtenburg, were enormous:

> By the end of 1932, American industry was operating at less than half its 1929 volume. For every four automobiles that had rolled off the assembly line in 1929, only one was turned out in 1932. Construction of office buildings halted so abruptly that some were left with naked girders rusting in the open air. Foreign trade slumped: Merchant ships carried outbound cargoes worth $5.2 billion in 1929 but only $1.6 billion in 1932. Blue-chip stocks fell, U.S. Steel from 262 to 22. American Can from 182 to 30. As crop prices plunged, many a farmer saw the labor of a lifetime wiped out and his fields, his house and his equipment put under the sheriff's hammer [sold at auction]. There were more than 13 million unemployed—a staggering 25 per cent of the labor force.[40]

The biggest difference between Roosevelt and Hoover was Roosevelt's determination that the federal government could—and should— alleviate American suffering. He felt it was the duty of the federal government to effect swift and widespread change to reverse the course of the still-declining economy. On Hoover's last day in office, he reportedly told an aide, "We are at the end of our rope. There is nothing more we can do."[41] Roosevelt disagreed.

Roosevelt's inaugural speech, delivered to a crowd of one hundred thousand gathered on the Capitol Plaza in Washington, DC, on March 4, 1933, and to tens of millions by radio, restored hope to the American people, while also telling them the recovery would be neither easy nor quick:

> This is preeminently the time to speak the truth, the whole truth, frankly and boldly. Nor need we shrink from honestly facing

conditions in our country today. This great nation will endure as it has endured, will revive, and will prosper. So, first of all, let me assert my firm belief that the only thing we have to fear is fear itself—nameless, unreasoning unjustified terror which paralyzes needed efforts to convert retreat into advance. . . .

The people of the United States have not failed. In their need they have registered a mandate that they want direct, vigorous action. They have asked for discipline and direction under leadership. They have made me the present instrument of their wishes. In the spirit of the gift I take it.[42]

The First One Hundred Days

Within a week, Roosevelt received half a million letters from Americans, expressing gratitude for his determination to turn the country away from economic collapse and toward the hope of restoring prosperity. During his first week, Roosevelt tackled what he deemed the most important of his plans for recovery—rehabilitation of the nation's banking system. The day after the inauguration, he called a special session of Congress and declared a national bank holiday, closing all banks throughout the country. The Emergency Banking Relief Act was introduced in Congress to reorganize the banking system. Accepted unanimously by the House, it passed the Senate with a vote of seventy-three to seven and was signed into law by 8:00 p.m.

The special session lasted one hundred days—March 9 through mid-June. Fourteen more laws were passed and implemented, addressing a wide range of problems. These included the creation of jobs through the Civilian Conservation Corps (CCC), which authorized 250,000 jobs for men aged eighteen to twenty-five; the building of dams to provide electricity to the Tennessee River Valley regions of Tennessee, North Carolina, Kentucky, Virginia, Mississippi, Georgia, and Alabama; legalizing the sale of beer containing up to 3.2 percent alcohol while the Eighteenth Amendment—repealing prohibition—was being ratified; and the creation of the Federal Deposit Insurance Corporation (FDIC) to insure depositors' money up to $500 when banks reopened.

Civilian Conservation Corps workers build a road on national forest land in northern California. President Franklin D. Roosevelt's New Deal programs created hundreds of thousands of jobs for struggling Americans who had lost their jobs in the Great Depression.

Never before had the federal government played such a large role in the everyday lives of citizens. President Hoover once declared that no American citizen would accept a government handout—that they would be insulted by the very idea. However, with the Depression threatening to devastate the country indefinitely, American citizens not only accepted government aid, they did so with a sense of hope. For the first time since the crash, they felt optimistic about the future, knowing it would take a long time for the nation to recover.

Tough Times for the Middle Class

There would be many ups and downs during the rest of the 1930s. The well-to-do suffered few changes in their lifestyles during the decade, while the very poor, who had been poor before the destruction of the economy, continued lives of poverty. The middle class suffered more. The lives they enjoyed during the 1920s were gone because of the loss of jobs. Those who felt their futures were bright with promise before the crash were suddenly dropped into the despair of the unemployed.

Wives and children also looked for work. Since women's jobs were not considered appropriate for men—such as cleaning houses or teaching school—there were times when women were able to find work but their husbands were not. Demoralized husbands were reduced to begging for jobs. Some abandoned their families, thinking their wives and children might qualify for relief more easily if they had no man to take care of them.

On the Dole

Most people reduced to seeking relief payments from the government were reluctant to ask for help, but when they could not feed their families or keep them warm, there were few alternatives. For increasing numbers of hungry people, the soup kitchens and bread lines—serving centers set up by charitable or civic organizations to feed the homeless and unemployed—became their only source of food. In many cities, lines of desperate people waiting to get a piece of bread or a cup of soup sometimes extended for blocks.

When local charities ran out of resources and were unable to continue feeding people, the only alternative was to apply for government relief. Those who qualified for the dole—a nickname for government relief—were sometimes described as listless, indifferent, lethargic, and docile. They had given up trying to support their families. They were without hope. Women wrote to First Lady Eleanor Roosevelt, begging her to send them clothes. Men often shared clothes with their children, taking turns wearing them. Women often took rags and made new clothes for themselves and their children. They made do with whatever they had, or they did without.

Grocery stores sometimes carried tabs for families when they could no longer purchase food with the small amount of money they earned.

Alphabet Agencies

From Roosevelt's first days in office through the 1930s, the president and Congress created about one hundred new government agencies aimed at creating jobs, providing safeguards against future financial crises, and stimulating the nation's economy. These agencies, part of Roosevelt's New Deal programs, were nicknamed Alphabet Agencies—or sometimes Alphabet Soup—because of the acronyms each was given. Among the agencies that were created, two stand out—the Civilian Conservation Corps (CCC) and the Works Progress Administration, later renamed the Works Projects Administration (WPA)—because they created badly needed jobs for people who had been unable to find them.

The CCC, created in 1933, provided 250,000 jobs for younger men, aged eighteen to twenty-five. By 1941 the CCC had planted more than 3 billion trees, built thousands of fire towers and almost one hundred thousand miles of roads, and had spent millions of man-hours fighting fires and floods across the country.

The WPA, created in 1935, employed an estimated 8.5 million Americans, mostly above the age of twenty-five, during its seven years of existence. The brainchild of Roosevelt's adviser Harry Hopkins, the agency worked on the premise that paid work was more beneficial to the unemployed than government handouts. In all, WPA workers participated in 1.4 million public work projects, including the construction or repair of thousands of golf courses, hospitals, airports, schools, parks, sports stadiums, playgrounds, buildings, and highways. The WPA also sponsored extensive fine arts, drama, and literacy projects.

In Seminole, Texas, Cora Marbut George ran a small grocery store. During the 1930s she somehow managed to feed the people in her small community, keeping records of what each family owed. Eventually, every penny was repaid. Cora would not allow children to starve.

Other children were not so fortunate. At the height of the Depression, a teacher in West Virginia recognized the symptoms of malnutrition in one of her students. She told the girl to go home and eat something. Her reply: "I can't. This is my sister's day to eat."[43]

Suffer the Children

During the Depression, children suffered alongside their parents, but they did not fully understand what had happened. Many no doubt wondered what had happened to change their lives so dramatically. Children often went to school with cardboard in their shoes to cover holes in the soles. Christmas was just another day. There was no money for gifts, nor was there money to buy materials to make gifts. During the 1930s children of the unemployed sometimes sent their Santa letters to FDR instead. In 1935 a ten-year-old Ohio girl wrote, "We have no one to give us a Christmas present, and if you want to buy a Christmas present please buy us a stove to do our cooking and to make good bread."[44]

Poorest of the Poor

Among the vast number of unemployed, one group of Americans suffered more than others. Black Americans had always been the first to be fired, the first to have wages or hours cut, and the last to be helped. Because of rampant racial discrimination in the South at the time—including harsh Jim Crow laws that guaranteed second-class treatment for blacks—Roosevelt was fairly limited as to what government programs he could propose that would help blacks as well as whites. He could not risk angering southerners and potentially lose their votes in Congress. Later, however, Eleanor became an advocate for black Americans' plight, doing what she could to alleviate their 50 percent unemployment and to fight discrimination. In a 1934 speech, she said the "day of selfishness" was over. "The day of working together has come, and we must learn to work together, all of us, regardless of race or creed or color. . . . We go ahead together or we go down together."[45]

All through the 1930s the unemployed or meagerly employed in cities across the nation suffered. But another group of Americans—those who lived in a region of the nation's heartland that came to be known as the Dust Bowl—suffered more than just the deprivation of economic collapse. They also lived through the most devastating natural disaster ever experienced in the United States.

Chapter 4

The Dirty Thirties

The Dust Bowl was an area of the southern plains that suffered the worst effects of drought in the 1930s. It included far-southern Nebraska, the western half of Kansas, southeastern Colorado, the Oklahoma panhandle, far-northeastern New Mexico, and the Texas panhandle. Areas north and south of the Dust Bowl also suffered from the drought—western and central Texas, the remainder of Oklahoma, New Mexico, Colorado, and Kansas, and farther north into the Dakotas and Canada. The worst dust storms blew all the way to the East Coast, dumping tons of dust and dirt on Chicago and New York City.

Avis D. Carson, who experienced Dust Bowl days firsthand, wrote about the endless sandstorms they called "dusters" in a 1935 article:

> The impact is like a shovelful of fine sand flung against the face. People caught in their own yards grope for the doorstep. Cars come to a standstill, for no light in the world can penetrate that swirling murk. . . . The nightmare is deepest during the storms. But on the occasional bright day and the usual gray day we cannot shake from it. We live with the dust, eat it, sleep with it, watch it strip us of possessions and the hope of possessions. It is becoming Real. The poetic uplift of spring fades into a phantom of the storied past. The nightmare is becoming life.[46]

The Great Plow-Up

Farmers were already struggling when the drought set in. The economic boom they enjoyed during World War I declined after the war, when wheat was no longer needed to support the war effort. Encouraged by high prices during wartime, many farmers mortgaged their farms to buy more land, which they cleared to plant more wheat. The grasslands of the Great Plains were destroyed by plows pulled by tractors, new mechanized vehicles that allowed farmers to plow many more acres per day than they could do with horse-drawn plows. Native Americans had warned "sod-busters"—an often derogatory term for farmers—not to kill the native grasses of the plains. These grasses held topsoil in place and had provided grazing land for millions of bison in the past. But money to be made selling wheat kept farmers focused on profits, even when the price of wheat dropped to the point of being worth less than the cost of growing it.

By October 1929 farmers were deep in debt and getting less for their crops each year. Then came the drought. Rain refused to fall for weeks or months at a time. With the prairie sod gone and topsoil exposed to dry winds moving across arid lands, severe dust storms of the "Dirty Thirties," as plains residents called them, swept away in minutes the topsoil that had taken millennia to accumulate. The dusters, sometimes growing to a height of more than two miles, scoured everything in their paths.

Black Sunday

Those who lived through the 1930s agree that the worst storm ever to attack the plains came on April 14, 1935—Black Sunday. The day dawned in the northern Texas panhandle, clear and sunny. People cleaned their houses, opened windows to let in clear, warm air, and went outside to enjoy the rare and precious day. Clothes were washed and hung outside to dry. Dust was shoveled off roofs, and sunshine shone through clean windows into houses that had not seen sunlight in months. The day gave everyone hope that the worst of the drought was over.

The year before—1934—had seen fifty-six dusters hit the area. January, February, and March of 1935 had seen only thirteen dust-free days. Beginning March 1, a duster had appeared every day for thirty straight days. The Red Cross had declared a medical emergency across the plains, dealing with cases of dust pneumonia. (When enough dust accumulated in a person's lungs, dust pneumonia occurred, with a mortality rate of 60 percent. The very young and the elderly succumbed most often, but no one was safe from it.) But maybe now Great Plains residents could look forward to the future again. Maybe this perfect day was an omen of better times to come. But it was not to be.

Early on that perfect plains day, a high pressure system over North and South Dakota met a cold front from the Yukon in Canada. This collision of warm and cold air produced violent winds that moved southwest over the grasslands, dropping temperatures by thirty degrees. By midmorning, the winds, which gathered dirt and dust as they roared over plowed land, entered Nebraska. By the time the storm reached Kansas, it was more than 200 miles (321.8 km) wide, with winds blowing 65 miles per hour (104.6 kph). Rabbits, birds, and other animals fled before the approaching storm. Static electricity from roiling dust stalled

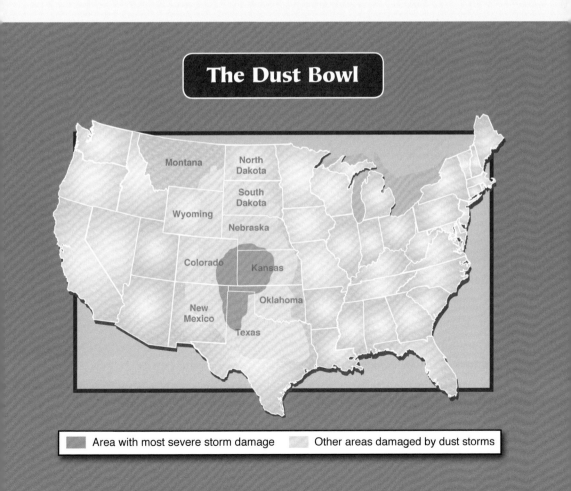

The Dust Bowl

Area with most severe storm damage   Other areas damaged by dust storms cars, interrupted radio reception, and knocked people down if they tried to shake hands. Barbed wire fences glowed with static electricity.

By the time the monstrous storm approached the area called No Man's Land, the area of the western part of the Oklahoma panhandle and the northern part of the Texas panhandle, it was after five o'clock in the evening. The storm appeared first as a black cloud on the horizon. Having seen these clouds many times before, parents shouted to their families, warning them to get inside. Within minutes, the storm was upon them, blotting out all sunlight, suffocating them if they could not get a handkerchief, sleeve, or skirt over their faces so they could breathe while running for shelter.

Melt White, from Dalhart, Texas, describes how dark it got when the storm hit:

> We was livin' in an old house that was 14 feet wide, and 36 feet long, just one room, board and batten with a washed roof on it. It kept gittin' darker and darker. And the old house was just a-vibratin' like it was gonna blow away. And I started tryin' to see my hand. And I kept bringin' my hand up closer and closer and closer and closer and closer and I finally touched the end of my nose and I still couldn't see my hand. That's how black it was.[47]

Battling Dusters

Plains residents tried to seal their homes against the insidious dust by gluing windows shut and draping wet sheets across doorways and windows to catch dust that seemed to seep through walls and window panes. Wet sheets were draped over baby cribs to keep dust away from infants. But no matter what they tried, dust managed to penetrate, leaving piles on everything inside. Each morning, a daily chore in most plains homes was to go room to room and scoop dust into buckets to be thrown outside. A long-time resident of Dalhart, Texas, Judge Wilson Cowen, tells interviewers:

The farmhouses looked terrible—the dust was deposited clear up to the window sills in these farmhouses, clear up to the window sills. And even about half of the front door was blocked by this sand. And if people inside wanted to get out, they had to climb out through the window to get out with a shovel to shovel out the front door. And, ah, there was no longer any yard at all there, not a green sprig, not a living thing of any kind, not even a field mouse. Nothing.[48]

Dust coated clothes, bedding, furniture, and every exposed inch of skin. The size of dust particles made them impossible to keep out. The printed period at the end of a typed sentence measures three hundred microns in diameter. The dust particles of the 1930s measured, at most, only sixty-three microns. Nothing could prevent such tiny particles from penetrating even the best-constructed homes.

An Oklahoma farmer's wife, Caroline Henderson, wrote a letter on June 30, 1935, describing her experiences near Shelton. In 1930 hail had destroyed their wheat crop. In 1931 low prices had undercut a reasonably successful crop. Then came years of drought. "There are days when for hours at a time we cannot see the windmill fifty feet from the kitchen door," she wrote. "There are days when for briefer periods one cannot distinguish the windows from the solid wall because of the solid blackness of the raging storm."[49]

In her letter, Henderson also hints at the feeling of hopelessness these dust storms engendered:

In the dust-covered desolation of our No Man's Land here, wearing our shade hats, with handkerchiefs tied over our faces and Vaseline in our nostrils, we have been trying to rescue our home from the wind-blown dust which penetrates wherever air can go. It is almost a hopeless task, for there is rarely a day when at some time the dust clouds do not roll over. "Visibility" approaches zero and everything is covered again with a silt-like deposit which may vary in depth from a film to actual ripples on the kitchen floor.[50]

The Great Plains Shelterbelt

President Roosevelt, in 1934, ordered the planting of 107,000 acres (43,301 ha) in a dead corner of Kansas, attempting to create a new ecosystem where the previous one had been utterly destroyed. Planted there were native plants, African grasses, blue grama, bluestem, buffalo grass, and other plants known to secure the soil. But it could take between ten and fifty years for the plains sod to be restored. Wanting to accomplish something faster, Roosevelt sent crews to plant trees in a line 100 miles (161 km) wide, from the Canadian border to just south of Amarillo, Texas. A team of eleven men could plant six thousand trees in one day. They began planting rows north to south, then switched to rows planted east to west, which proved to be a more effective wind barrier.

The strips were planted up to a mile (1.6 km) apart, with one hundred strips within what Roosevelt called the Great Plains Shelterbelt. Farming could be done between the strips. Cottonwoods, honey locusts, hackberries, ash, walnuts, ponderosa pines, and Chinese elms were planted—and survived the winter. Encouraged, Roosevelt continued with his goal of planting 180,000 trees a year on private lands, with owners agreeing to take care of the saplings. By 1942, an estimated 220 million trees had been planted. Although most of the trees were later cut down to once again open more land for cultivation, some of the Shelterbelt trees remain on the Great Plains, helping prevent erosion.

Breathing dust became a way of life, sometimes leading to coughing so severe that ribs broke. Imogene Glover, of Guymon, Oklahoma, in that state's panhandle, relates:

When those dust storms blew and you were out in 'em, it would just coat the inside of your nose literally. And sometimes your mouth would just get cottony dry because, well, you spit out dirt sometimes. It looked like tobacco juice, only it was dirt, when you'd spit.[51]

Farm Foreclosures

With severe drought came destruction of crops and livestock from dusters. Cattle and horses dropped dead, with dust packing their eyes, noses, and lungs until they could no longer see or breathe. Carcasses, when cut open, revealed large balls of mud in their stomachs. Banks foreclosed on farms when loans could not be repaid, and farmsteads were auctioned. With few buyers able to pay full price, banks were willing to risk selling the property at auction. That at least ensured a return on a portion of what they had loaned farmers when they had financed their land. Often, however, neighbors would agree not to bid on a farm, so that its owners could bid on their own land and buy it back from the bank for much less than the market price.

T.H. Watkins describes how neighbors—and sometimes complete strangers—came together to help farmers who could not pay their mortgages and faced losing everything they had worked years, or generations, to build. When the bidding began:

Someone in the crowd would start it off at fifteen cents or so, and it rarely got beyond a few dollars before the bidding stopped and the auctioneer would close the sale. If anyone in the farmyard might be so ignorant of what was going on as to put in a serious bid, a suitably burly man would be likely to step up and put a hand on his shoulders with the words, "That bid's a little high, ain't it?" So it was that in the fall of 1932 an $800 mortgage on Walter Crozier's farm outside Haskins, Iowa, was satisfied for $1.90, or that the horses, cows and chickens offered for sale at Theresa Von Baum's farm near Elgin, Nebraska, went back to her at a nickel apiece, for a total of $5.35.[52]

A fearsome, roiling dust storm overtakes homes in Stratford, Texas, in April 1935. Dust storms like this one swept away precious topsoil from farmland all across the plains states. People's health suffered, too, as the thick dust accumulated in their lungs.

Some farm states enacted moratoria on farm foreclosures. Still, by 1932, a third of plains farmers faced foreclosure because they could not pay their taxes or their debts. They were forced to live in tents or to move away and live with relatives.

Black Blizzards

The Black Blizzards, as these monster dust storms were called, kept people in complete darkness for more than an hour. When it was possible to see again and go outside, everyone's face was black and muddied with tears. People described the utter blackness as the blackest of blacks, "like the inside of a dog." Pulitzer prize–winning author Timothy Egan describes how one such storm left the town of Dalhart, Texas:

> The storm left the streets full of coal-colored dust and covered the tops of cars and the sidewalks. . . . The dust found the insides, too, coating the dining table and wood floor of Doc Dawson's place, and the fine furniture inside the DeSoto [Hotel] lobby, and the pool tables at Dinwiddie's, and the baseball stands at the edge of town. Folks had it in their hair, their eyes, down their throat. You blew your nose and there it was—black snot. You hacked up the same thing. It burned your eyes and made people cough. It was the damnedest thing.[53]

The speed of the winds was estimated to have reached 100 miles per hour (160.9 kph) at the uppermost crest of the storm, and at least 60 miles per hour (96.6 kph) on the ground. The farther the storm went, the slower it got, until at dusk it was moving only 40 miles per hour (64.4 kph). By the next day the storm had carried tons of Great Plains topsoil hundreds of miles—all the way to the Gulf of Mexico.

Conservation Efforts

On April 19, 1935, five days after Black Sunday, Hugh Hammond Bennett, an expert on soil conservation, was in Washington, DC, trying to convince congressmen to enact legislation to conserve whatever topsoil was left in the plains while there was still enough soil to support farming. His pleas were ignored. The congressmen had never seen anything like Bennett described, so they had no frame of reference. Partway through his presentation, one of Bennett's aides whispered to him that proof was on the way. Bennett kept talking another hour, until the sky in Washington, DC, began to dim.

One senator interrupted him to point out that it was getting dark outside—in the middle of the day. As the sky darkened, topsoil from the Great Plains drifted onto the nation's capital by the ton. "This, gentlemen," Bennett told the incredulous congressmen staring in awe out the windows of the Senate Office Building, "is what I'm talking about. There goes Oklahoma."[54]

Within a day, Bennett had funds for conservation. Congress passed the Soil Conservation Act, which was the first such act in the nation's history. Efforts began in earnest to do something about the ruined plains, where an estimated 850 million tons (771 million metric tons) of topsoil had blown away in 1935 alone. Congressmen and President Roosevelt set their minds to finding ways to reverse this disastrous situation.

Plagues of Locusts

In the spring of 1937 the government gave away grass seed and paid farmers to plant it. They were also encouraged to try new methods of soil conservation, such as abandoning the straight rows they had always plowed in favor of terracing and curved rows, to minimize the amount of soil that would be carried by wind. Windbreaks, rows of drought-resistant trees planted to diminish the erosion and raise humidity levels, were planted across the plains.

Roosevelt's and Bennett's conservation efforts eventually helped rehabilitate much of the plains, but it could not be accomplished overnight. In 1937 more dusters came, and summer brought temperatures of more than 110°F (43.3° C). Grasshoppers moved in huge clouds, devouring virtually everything in their paths. An estimated twenty-three thousand grasshoppers per acre (0.4 ha), 14 million per square mile (2.6 sq km), were coming from the dry Rocky Mountains in search of food. The National Guard killed grasshoppers by burning fields, poisoning them, and dragging rollers behind tractors to crush them. Mounds of grasshoppers piled up against fences and houses.

The Great Move Westward

Just after the crash in 1929, officials of the Missouri Pacific Railroad reported that over 13,000 people had "hopped a freight"—ridden a train without buying a ticket. Two years later, the railroad company estimated there were nearly 190,000 people riding free. Two years after that, their

"Big Rabbit Drive Sunday— Bring Clubs"

One of the most destructive pests facing the plains during the 1930s was the never-ending onslaught of jackrabbits that invaded homes and destroyed crops. They came by the thousands, eating everything, including a little girl's doll left in the yard of one house in the Texas panhandle.

In 1932 John McCarty, editor of the Dalhart *Texan*, decided to rid the town of rabbits. He announced a round-up, and a horde of local residents gathered to help. Author Timothy Egan describes the event:

> People gathered in a fenced field at the edge of Dalhart, about two thousand folks armed with baseball bats and clubs. The atmosphere was festive, many people drinking corn whiskey from jugs. At last, they were about to do *something*, striking a blow against this run of freakish nature. They spread to the edge of the fenced section, forming a perimeter, then moved toward the center, herding rabbits inward to a staked enclosure. As the human noose tightened, rabbits hopped around madly, sniffing the air, stumbling over each other. The clubs smashed heads. The bats crushed rib cages. Blood splattered, teeth were knocked out, hair was matted and reddened. The rabbits panicked, screamed. It took most of an afternoon to crush several thousand rabbits. Their bodies were left in a bloodied heap at the center of the field. Somebody strung up a few hundred of them and took a picture.

Rabbit drives continued, sometimes weekly, but were never sufficient to stop the hordes of hungry hares.

Timothy Egan, *The Worst Hard Time: The Untold Story of Those Who Survived the Great American Dust Bowl.* New York: Houghton Mifflin, 2006, p. 116.

estimate was over a million. These Americans—on the move, looking for work or a handout—were considered transients. Whether by rail, car, hitchhiking, or on foot, people from the Great Plains left their farms by the thousands each month in search of a better life. Many moved west to California, hoping for work, and to escape the dust.

According to the US Census, every state in the Dust Bowl lost population during the 1930s. Kansas lost 4 percent between the 1930 and the 1940 census, Nebraska 4 percent, North Dakota 3 percent, South Dakota 7 percent, and Oklahoma an astounding 18.4 percent. Not since the days of wagon trains crossing the plains had so many headed west in search of a fresh start. With cars loaded with whatever they could haul, entire families moved westward. No one knows exactly how many Americans became homeless during the Depression, but estimates run as high as 3.5 million. American author Milton Meltzer explains that not all transients were adults: "Many boys and girls who failed to find jobs near home or felt they were a burden to their parents simply took to the road. A sight new to the 1930s was the army of young transients. The Children's Bureau estimated that by late 1932 a quarter of a million under the age of twenty-one were roaming the country.[55]

Many who headed to California did not find what they were looking for. Instead of a new beginning, many faced ridicule, discrimination, and abuse at the hands of California farm owners and crew bosses. Watkins describes conditions for migrant workers in California:

Huddling to wait out off-season unemployment in makeshift "shack-towns" and "Little Oklahomas" perched on the outskirts of agricultural service centers like Bakersfield, Fresno, and Modesto, collecting state relief, sending their children to local schools, the migrants soon earned the pious contempt of their neighbors in the traditional manner of humans rejecting outsiders who are unfamiliar and therefore vaguely threatening. Whatever their origin, they became known as "Okies" and "Arkies," with a few "Texies" thrown in for good measure, and were subject to the kind of abuse and discrimination that the state's Mexican-American, Filipino, and African-American field workers had endured as a matter of course for decades.[56]

A migrant farmworker's wife sits for a moment with her children in a California migrant camp in 1936. The photograph, taken by famed photographer Dorothea Lange, captures the desperation and determination of those who sought to escape the Dust Bowl by heading west.

Roosevelt Tours the Dust Bowl

Roosevelt, while running for reelection in 1936, toured nine states devastated by drought and dust storms. On September 6, 1936, he addressed the nation in one of his "Fireside Chats," reporting what he had seen: "I shall never forget the fields of wheat so blasted by heat that they cannot be harvested. I shall never forget field after field of corn stunted, earless, and stripped of leaves, for what the sun left the grasshoppers took. I saw brown pastures which would not keep a cow on fifty acres."[57]

Never again would the high plains be the same. In some places the land healed, helped by soil conservation methods, while others remained scarred and lifeless. Altogether, the federal government purchased 11.3 million acres (4.6 million ha) of useless fields and attempted to restore them to grassland. After more than sixty-five years, some of that land is still sterile and barren, but animals once again graze most of the lands destroyed during the 1920s and 1930s. Within the heart of the Dust Bowl today are three national grasslands cared for by the US Forest Service. The largest of these is Comanche National Grassland, 440,000 acres (178,000 ha) in southeastern Colorado.

Of the nearly 220 million trees planted by Roosevelt, most are gone now. Some trees died from the drought that lingered years after they were planted, or during droughts that occurred during the decades following the "Dirty Thirties." Most, however, were destroyed when rains returned in the 1940s, wheat prices rose again, and farmers ripped out the Shelterbelt trees, plowing the ground to plant wheat.

End of Depression

Despite the best efforts of the federal government, the Great Depression continued throughout the decade of the 1930s. It took another war to bring the United States out of the Depression. When the nation entered World War II in 1941 the economy got the boost it needed. The country supported the war effort with increased production of food, weapons, ammunition, and other goods, just as it had during World War I.

National unity against a common foe brought the country together and got it back on its feet after more than ten years of economic depression and harsh weather conditions that had killed thousands, stolen hope from millions, and devastated the heartland of the nation. By this time, however, safeguards were in place that were intended to prevent such a depression from ever again gripping the nation.

Chapter 5

What Is the Legacy of the Great Depression?

On September 1, 1939, Nazi Germany invaded Poland, forcing Great Britain and France to declare war on Germany. World War II had begun. As the war wore on, so, too, did the devastation of Europe. Oddly enough, the early years of the war had the opposite effect on the United States economically. First, as a major supplier of the Allied war effort, the United States once again found markets for its surplus production. Food, clothing, medical supplies, vehicles such as airplanes and ships, weapons, and ammunition sold to the Allies brought American farms and factories back to life. Jobs were available once again. People who had been unemployed—some for years—found work.

Then in December 1941, when the Japanese attack on Pearl Harbor brought the United States into the conflict, thousands more enlisted. World War II brought the Great Depression to a close. Because of the war, the American people found purpose again. Chronic unemployment, bread lines, soup kitchens, riding the rails in search of work became memories for most. But elements and lessons of the Great Depression endured in the people who had lived through that dreadful decade.

"Make It Do, or Do Without"

During the Great Depression people lived by the adage: "Use it up, wear it out, make it do or do without."[58] They also learned to save every penny they could possibly save, and they were willing to do any kind of work, no matter how menial, if it meant putting food on the table. Eighty years later, those who lived during the 1930s are still saving their money, and many refuse to go into debt for any reason. If they do not have the money to pay for something in full, they do without it, or they save for it until they have the full cost. Some veterans of the Depression still do not fully trust banks to protect their money.

Depression folks are among the most frugal folks around. They still remove wrapping paper from gifts carefully, fold it, and save it to be used later. They stretch out their Thanksgiving turkey dinner by using every morsel, including cooking down the bones and scraps to make soup

Sailors in a small craft rescue a survivor beside the sunken battleship USS West Virginia *on December 7, 1941, in the Japanese attack on Pearl Harbor. The attack pushed the United States into World War II and helped lift the nation out of the Great Depression.*

stock. Catsup bottles will be perched upside down in the refrigerator, just to drain the last bits of catsup, and then the empty bottle may be rinsed and the catsup-tinged rinse water added to meatloaf, soup, or spaghetti sauce.

Alene George, a retired West Texas school teacher, is ninety-seven. She has ample income to buy whatever she needs but still squeezes every toothpaste tube until it is perfectly flat, then cuts the tube in half with scissors and uses a cotton swab to tease the last remaining toothpaste from the tube. Pauline Hudson, also from Texas, was asked by her niece why she always carefully scraped every last remnant of cake batter from the mixing bowl into the baking pan. Surely, it would be quicker and easier to throw out that last bit. After all, it was only a spoonful. But Hudson saw that last spoonful of batter as one more bite of cake. And during the Depression, that one bite of cake might have been hers.

Oral History, Sevier County, Utah

In December 1997 high school students in Sevier County, Utah, were given an assignment to interview people in their county who had lived through the Great Depression, and to record the oral history they could gain from these people. Their interviews are now part of the New Deal Network, an online teaching and research project established in 1996 by the Franklin and Eleanor Roosevelt Institute (FERI), based at Columbia University.

Utah was hit especially hard during the Depression, because a majority of those living in the state during the 1930s were farmers. The unemployment rate in Utah in 1933 was 35.8 percent, and during the decade of the 1930s, the rate averaged 26 percent. The stories these people shared with the students matched those of other Depression survivors from across the country.

Those who were interviewed recommended that people learn to spend less and be thankful for whatever they have, instead of constantly wanting more. They adamantly recommended never going into debt and that everyone should save a little every month, no matter what

Roosevelt and the Modern Presidency

Roosevelt was the first president to make full use of broadcast media to share his ideas, his counsel, and his programs directly with the American people. Over the space of a dozen years—from March 12, 1933, until June 12, 1944—Roosevelt addressed the nation by radio in what became known as "Fireside Chats." His openness, speaking in direct, simple language, served to comfort and give hope to people in times of crisis.

Presidents since Roosevelt have continued his practice, either through press conferences or direct addresses to the American people, usually from the Oval Office. Truman addressed the nation about the atomic bomb in 1945. Eisenhower talked about racial violence that erupted outside Little Rock, Arkansas, schools in 1957. Kennedy reassured the nation during the Cuban Missile Crisis in 1962, Reagan spoke about the space shuttle *Challenger* explosion in 1986, and George W. Bush consoled Americans after the 9/11 attacks.

their paychecks might be. And they agreed: Having to do without during the Depression made them stronger. Some consider it a blessing. They learned to work, be productive, and help support their families. Lessons in frugality have lasted throughout their lives. More than anything, they appreciate what they have now a lot more than they would if they had not lived through the Depression.

One Richfield interviewee, eighty-seven-year-old Cherril Ogden, gave the following advice: "Be careful how you spend your money . . . so if there's a shortage of money you'll know what's important to buy, not buy silly things, just 'cause they're mod and in. And then, stay close to your family, stay close to your church, and hold on to religion."[59] Many survivors say that praying to God for strength to get through hard times was sometimes their only comfort. Ninety-one-year-old Morris Ogden, another Richfield citizen, adds, "Look ahead. Don't wait until your last penny is gone before you say, Oh no! We're out of coal or wood. Save your money for a rainy day, don't spend it foolishly, buy what you need, save the rest."[60]

Lisa Nielsen, one of the students involved in the Sevier County Oral History Project, sums up what she and her fellow students learned from the project: "The Depression was a 'hard time.' Those who experienced it reflect upon it and come to this simple conclusion. However, they were able to grow and learn from it. This is true with any trial that may enter a person's life. It is important to take life experiences and learn from them all that they would teach us."[61]

Lessons Learned

The federal government was transformed by the Great Depression and the New Deal. Sitting back, watching so many US citizens struggle financially, and expecting sufficient help to come from families, churches, charitable organizations, communities, or states, did not keep the American people fed, nor did it get them back to work. Under the New Deal, the federal government took on new responsibilities to safeguard not only America, but American lives and livelihoods as well. Those responsibilities and promises to the American people have endured. The new role of support and care that was established during the 1930s continues in the twenty-first century.

During the early years of the Depression, President Hoover raised interest rates and taxes and rejected the idea of helping people through public assistance and relief programs. He and his administration denied that it was the government's obligation to feed hungry people and help them find jobs again. Hoover's policies failed.

Through trial and error, failure and success, those in the Roosevelt administrations learned what worked to help the economy through the Depression and what did not. After the 1930s, many economists believed that three New Deal strategies usually work to help pull a nation out of a recession or depression. First, lowered interest rates stimulate borrowing and investment. Second, increased spending by the government through public works projects, for example, and tax cuts to put cash into citizens' pockets give the national economy a boost. Third, maintaining and expanding programs designed as safety nets, such as welfare and unemployment insurance, help people through times of economic difficulty and help them support their families when they are out of work.

Each president who has served since FDR, be he conservative Republican or liberal Democrat, has looked at New Deal programs differently. Some of Roosevelt's programs have been discarded, but some—like Social Security, FDIC-insured bank deposits, and unemployment insurance—have remained, becoming permanent fixtures. Each president has recognized the importance of maintaining these social and economic safeguards for the nation's citizens.

Whether a person looks favorably on what Roosevelt and the New Deal did to transform the country or believes his programs will eventually prove to be damaging, Watkins comments that:

> Many of the bridges we cross in our automobiles today were built during the New Deal. The vegetables and fruit we put on our tables most of the time were grown on land irrigated by water stored behind a dam constructed during the New Deal—and any one of those dams could also be producing the light by which this book is being read. Much of our urban sewerage is still being treated in sanitation plants given us by the New Deal. Much of our tap water and natural gas come to our homes via pipes laid by the New Deal. We are still driving around on country highways first paved by the New Deal, camping in national parks and national monuments established by the New Deal, strolling on national forest hiking trails laid out by the New Deal under a canopy of trees planted by the New Deal, swimming in public pools built by the New Deal, mailing our letters in post offices constructed by the New Deal, getting marriage licenses in city halls erected with New Deal money. We are still sued in New Deal courthouses, educated in New Deal schools, get well or die in New Deal hospitals, and live in New Deal urban housing projects.

The legacy of the New Dealers, then, is infrastructure as well as politics and government—and if a good deal of it is beginning to disintegrate in our own time, it still stands as the most permanent physical evidence we have of the power of the dreams that fired those people in that time.[62]

No Place Like Home!

Two movies released toward the end of the 1930s have become classics in American culture—*Gone with the Wind* and *The Wizard of Oz*—because of the way they capsulize sudden loss of security and the characters' struggles to put things right.

Gone with the Wind takes Scarlett O'Hara from her comfortable, enjoyable life at Tara, flirting with young men, falling in love with Ashley Wilkes, despising Rhett Butler, to seeing her world fall apart when the Civil War breaks out. Scarlett goes from financial security to abject poverty, just as many Americans did after the stock market crash. But through sheer determination and will, Scarlett returns to Tara, vowing to bring it back to its previous splendor. Her final remark, "Tomorrow is another day!" epitomizes the outlook of many Americans during the Depression years.

The Wizard of Oz has a similar theme. Dorothy's world is blown away by a tornado, which sweeps her into a strange land. When the stock market crashed, most Americans were thrust into a new world, where all the comforts of home slipped away. Dorothy is able to find her way to Oz—and then back to Kansas—with the help of friends, just as Depression folk received help from friends and family during hard times.

The same indomitable spirit each of these characters embodies endures today in America. The attacks of 9/11 and the latest economic recession have once again challenged the nation, but they have also rallied its citizens to persevere.

Social Services Established

Many of the social services created during Roosevelt's presidency continue to the present day. Federal and State Unemployment Compensation, for example, protect those out of work. This was part of the Social Security Act of 1935. Temporary Assistance for Needy Families (TANF) developed from the Aid to Dependent Children Act of 1935. The Housing Choice Voucher Program—enabling people to pay rent according to the amount of their income—came from a 1937 law known as Section 8. The Supplemental Nutrition Assistance Program, which issues food stamps to those who qualify, based on their income level, came from a New Deal program that ran from 1939 to 1943.

Roosevelt wanted to establish a program for national health care in 1935, but it lacked support in Congress and was defeated. In 1965 the push for national health care was revived, but again met stern resistance. The effort was reduced to the Medicaid and Medicare programs during President Lyndon Johnson's term. The next push for health care reform came in 1993, during President Bill Clinton's term.

Finally, in 2009, under President Barack Obama, the Patient Protection and Affordable Care Act (PPACA) was passed and signed into law. It was challenged by Republicans as unconstitutional. In June 2012 by a vote of five to four, the Supreme Court upheld all but one section of the law—the one that would penalize states for not expanding state-run Medicaid programs. In spite of this landmark decision, Republicans continue to oppose the law and work actively to abolish it. If the law survives, it is scheduled to be fully implemented by 2014.

Minimum Wage and Unions

Two important contributions to the US economy that came from the New Deal were the Fair Labor Standards Act of 1938, which established a federal minimum wage, and the development of organized labor. Both led to higher wages and better working conditions for millions in the nation's workforce. Increases in the minimum wage have never been a regular occurrence, but instead depend on the whims of Congress and the president for adjustments corresponding to the cost of living and inflation.

The result has been sporadic raises that are sometimes spread over years, in small increments. Between May 1974 and January 1976 the federal minimum wage increased three times. From February 1981 to March 1990, and between October 1997 and June 2007, there were no increases in the minimum wage at all. Minimum wage has never been sufficient to bring a family of four above the poverty line when only one family member is employed. States can choose to establish a minimum wage that is higher than the federal level, and by 2009 twenty-seven states had chosen to do so.

Organized labor unions tend to ignore minimum wage levels and negotiate their own levels, specific to their particular segment of the workforce. In 1945 unions boasted a membership constituting 35 percent of working Americans. By 2008 that number had declined to 12.4 percent. The majority of union members are among the public sector of the workforce rather than the private sector. The primary labor union until 2005 was the American Federation of Labor–Congress of Industrial Organizations (AFL-CIO). That year several member unions left the AFL-CIO to form Change to Win, taking 25 percent of AFL-CIO members into the new coalition.

Because of minimum wage laws and the actions of organized labor, American workers for the most part are no longer at the mercy of unfair employers who refuse to pay a decent wage. Programs established during the 1930s provide safeguards for American workers, but even today, those who work for minimum wage agree that the intention of providing a living wage for all workers has not yet been fully met.

Chronic Debt

One financial practice that first appeared in the 1920s and continues today is credit buying. Buying on credit, particularly with credit cards—which first appeared in the 1950s—has become a predominant theme of American life. Most Americans today have multiple cards and carry sometimes thousands of dollars of credit card debt. Recent decades have seen this economic practice mushroom. In 1978 a Supreme Court decision allowed banks to charge higher rates of interest. They could also solicit new customers in states other than the home state of the bank offering the cards.

From that point, the already high amount of debt in the United States rose exponentially, with banks making difficult-to-resist introductory offers of exceptionally low interest rates. Banks sometimes raised interest rates without notice and without providing reasons to the customer. American consumer debt in 1988, excluding residential mortgages, totaled $700 billion. By 2008 the total was a staggering $2.6 trillion.

When the 2007 recession hit, consumers finally started to limit credit buying. By that time, though, 14 percent of the average family's income went to payments on credit card debt. And, because the average family's debt is larger, their monthly payments are higher, typically leaving them with less cash available at the end of each month to put into savings accounts or other long-term investments.

Looking Back

Economists still debate the causes of the Great Depression. Most, however, agree on six key factors. First, overuse of credit buying, with little or no regulation, led to excessive consumer debt. Second was a massive maldistribution of wealth. During the 1920s the rich got richer, the poor remained poor, and the middle class became part of the poor.

Third, speculation in the stock market caused stock prices to soar, which encouraged investors to buy more stock on margin. When the collapse came, a substantial portion of the nation's capital disappeared from circulation. Fourth, the nation's banks lacked sufficient capital to weather an economic collapse. They had loaned too much without sufficient collateral, and there was little or no regulation on banking to require them to retain a reservoir of capital, should the worst happen. When the worst did happen, thousands of banks closed, taking their investors' money with them into bankruptcy.

The fifth cause of the Great Depression was the overproduction of goods. When the crash occurred, manufacturers stopped production and laid off workers. The country was glutted with products no one could afford to buy, and the nation's unemployment rate soared. The sixth cause of the Depression came from the federal government itself. Hoover, unsure of what steps to take, actually stifled the economy instead of stimulating it. Raising taxes and putting high tariffs on imported goods financially strangled individuals and companies alike. These actions also prevented European countries from selling their goods to the United States and using profits to repay World War I debt to the United States.

The consequences of these six factors led to a catastrophic economic meltdown. The ripple effect circled the globe. When the American economy failed, so did the economies of countries around the world. The policies implemented by Roosevelt, once he took office in March 1933, got the country moving again, slowly. If not for World War II, however, economists are unsure how much longer it would have taken to pull the country—and the world—out of the Depression.

Postwar Recessions

The question remained at the end of the Great Depression: Could such a disaster strike again? So far, the answer has been no, but Americans have peered over the brink several times in recessions that threatened the country with another economic meltdown. Since the end of World War II, according to economists, there have been eleven recessions. They took place during the term of Harry Truman in 1948, Dwight Eisenhower in 1953, 1957, and 1960, Richard Nixon in 1969 and 1973, Jimmy Carter in 1980, Ronald Reagan in 1981, George H.W. Bush in 1990, and George W. Bush in 2001 and 2007.

The recession that occurred in 2007 has earned the nickname "The Great Recession." It lasted nineteen months (despite the fact that its effects were felt a lot longer), and between December 2007 and March 2009 the stock market lost almost 50 percent of its value. US unemployment reached 8.1 percent, and the gross domestic product dropped

2.2 percent. The Great Recession was the closest the United States has come to falling into another depression, and it is considered the worst economic slump since the 1930s.

The nation was saved from economic collapse during each of the post-Depression recessions, but the threat of repeating the disaster of the 1930s as a result of the Great Recession shook government leaders and Americans to the core. Thankfully, safeguards, many created in the 1930s, have so far held firm, and the social programs put in place during that decade once again have helped people in need.

Into the Future

When the Great Depression ended, millions of Americans breathed a collective sigh of relief that was felt around the world. The United States finally raised its head and looked forward to renewed prosperity. World

Hundreds of people wait in line for a job fair in California in 2009. US unemployment, home foreclosures, and business failures soared during the Great Recession—the closest the United States has come to falling into a ruinous depression like the one that took place in the 1930s.

JOB FAIR

War II would claim countless American lives, but those who survived carried with them what they had learned during the Great Depression and tried to pass along these lessons to future generations.

According to Watkins, when Americans faced World War II in late 1941, they "came to the challenge well armed":

Agonies of personal financial devastation and the social, political, and economic programs of the New Deal had combined to produce a world in which the great hope of true democracy had lurched a little closer to reality; in which women, people of color, people of no previous standing in the pantheon of progress, had acquired some measure of power; in which labor had been raised up to challenge capital more effectively than ever before; and in which government and the people to be governed were newly bound in an intimacy that would never be diminished. This new world would soon be tested by war and would prove itself not merely durable, but enduring.[63]

During the Great Depression, many people agree, the following lessons were learned: that, in times of crisis, the federal government has the *responsibility* to come to the aid of individual American citizens, that all Americans *should* work together for the common good, that we each *are* our brothers' (and sisters') keeper, and that together, there is *little* the nation cannot accomplish. These lessons are still a part of American life, no matter how hard the frenetic pace of daily life and the nation's petty political, social, and philosophical differences try to erase them.

During Roosevelt's presidency—and for decades since—there have been widely different opinions about how he dealt with the Great Depression. His New Deal programs forever altered the relationship between individual American citizens and their federal government, and not everyone agrees that the change was a good one. Many today consider Roosevelt the nation's savior in a time of extreme hardship, putting him on a par with Abraham Lincoln and his preservation of the Union despite the American Civil War. Others, however, believe Roosevelt's New Deal programs, with their insinuation into Americans' private lives and their high price tags, have actually saddled the nation with massive and undesirable financial and social burdens.

Roosevelt and the New Deal transformed the United States. And, for good or bad, the nation today is what the Great Depression, the New Deal, and World War II made it. As Watkins so simply and elegantly describes the connection between today's American citizens and those who endured the Great Depression, "What we are is what they became."[64]

Source Notes

Introduction: The Defining Characteristics of the Great Depression

1. Quoted in Studs Terkel, *Hard Times: An Oral History of the Great Depression*. New York: New Press, 1970, 1986, p. 20.
2. Quoted in Terkel, *Hard Times*, pp. 20–21.
3. T.H. Watkins, *The Great Depression: America in the 1930s*. New York: Back Bay/Little, Brown, 1993, p. 13.
4. Watkins, *The Great Depression: America in the 1930s*, p. 12.
5. Watkins, *The Great Depression: America in the 1930s*, p. 12.
6. MedicineNet.com, "Definition of Depression." www.medterms.com.

Chapter One: What Conditions Led to the Great Depression?

7. Ernest R. May and Editors of Time-Life Books, *Boom and Bust*, vol. 10 of *The LIFE History of the United States: 1917–1932*. New York: Time-Life, 1974, p. 150.
8. Robert S. McElvaine, *The Great Depression: America, 1929–1941*. New York: Three Rivers, 2009, p. 13.
9. May and Editors of Time-Life Books, *Boom and Bust*, p. 102.
10. McElvaine, *The Great Depression: America, 1929–1941*, p. 17.
11. Frederick Lewis Allen, *Only Yesterday: An Informal History of the 1920's*. New York: First Perennial Classics/HarperCollins, 2000, p. 68.
12. Quoted in Cyndy Bittinger, "The Business of America Is Business?," Calvin Coolidge Memorial Foundation. www.calvin-coolidge.org.
13. McElvaine, *The Great Depression: America, 1929–1941*, p. 14.
14. John Kenneth Galbraith, *The Great Crash, 1929*. New York: Houghton Mifflin Harcourt, 2009, p. 3.

15. McElvaine, *The Great Depression: America, 1929–1941*, p. 41.

16. McElvaine, *The Great Depression: America, 1929–1941*, p. 13.

17. Watkins, *The Great Depression: America in the 1930s*, p. 38.

18. Galbraith, *The Great Crash, 1929*, p. 22.

Chapter Two: Ignoring the Signs

19. Galbraith, *The Great Crash, 1929*, p. 25.

20. McElvaine, *The Great Depression: America, 1929–1941*, p. 46.

21. Quoted in Allen, *Only Yesterday*, p. 263.

22. Galbraith, *The Great Crash, 1929*, p. 26.

23. Quoted in Galbraith, *The Great Crash 1929*, p. 37.

24. Watkins, *The Great Depression: America in the 1930s*, p. 39.

25. Steve Wiegand, *Lessons from the Great Depression for Dummies*. Hoboken, NJ: Wiley, 2009, p. 23.

26. Quoted in Galbraith, *The Great Crash, 1929*, pp. 84–85.

27. Galbraith, *The Great Crash, 1929*, p. 88.

28. Quoted in Allen, *Only Yesterday*, p. 281.

29. Quoted in Allen, *Only Yesterday*, p. 281.

30. Quoted in Allen, *Only Yesterday*, pp. 281–82.

31. Galbraith, *The Great Crash, 1929*, p. 99.

32. Quoted in Galbraith, *The Great Crash, 1929*, p. 107.

Chapter Three: From Bad to Worse

33. Quoted in Wiegand, *Lessons from the Great Depression for Dummies*, p. 58.

34. Quoted in Wiegand, *Lessons from the Great Depression for Dummies*, p. 70.

35. Wiegand, *Lessons from the Great Depression for Dummies*, p. 70.

36. H. Paul Jeffers, *The Complete Idiot's Guide to the Great Depression*. Indianapolis, IN: Alpha, 2002, p. 48.

37. Watkins, *The Great Depression: America in the 1930s*, pp. 60–61.

38. Quoted in Jeffers, *The Complete Idiot's Guide to the Great Depression*, pp. 61–62.

39. Quoted in Jeffers, *The Complete Idiot's Guide to the Great Depression*, p. 64.

40. William E. Leuchtenburg and Editors of Time-Life Books, *New Deal and War*, vol. 11 of *The LIFE History of the United States: 1933–1945*. New York: Time-Life Books, 1974, pp. 7–8.

41. Quoted in Jeffers, *The Complete Idiot's Guide to the Great Depression*, p. 71.

42. Quoted in Robert Torricelli and Andrew Carroll, eds., *In Our Own Words: Extraordinary Speeches of the American Century*. New York: Kodansha International, 1999, pp. 100–101.

43. Quoted in Wiegand, *Lessons from the Great Depression for Dummies*, p. 59.

44. Quoted in McElvaine, *The Great Depression: America, 1929–1941*, p. 185.

45. Quoted in McElvaine, *The Great Depression: America, 1929-1941*, p. 191.

Chapter Four: The Dirty Thirties

46. Quoted in PBS, "Black Sunday: April 14, 1935," *American Experience: Surviving the Dust Bowl*, August 16, 2011. www.pbs.org.

47. Quoted in PBS, "Black Sunday: April 14, 1935."

48. Quoted in PBS, "Black Sunday: April 14, 1935."

49. Quoted in Watkins, *The Great Depression: America in the 1930s*, p. 189.

50. Quoted in Timothy Egan, *The Worst Hard Time: The Untold Story of Those Who Survived the Great American Dust Bowl*. New York: Houghton Mifflin, 2006, p. 257.

51. Quoted in PBS, "Black Sunday."

52. Watkins, *The Great Depression: America in the 1930s*, p. 119.

53. Egan, *The Worst Hard Time*, p. 114.

54. Quoted in Egan, *The Worst Hard Time*, p. 228.

55. Quoted in Judy Busk, "Migration: The Theme of the Great Depression," Always Lend a Helping Hand, New Deal Network. http://newdeal.feri.org.

56. Watkins, *The Great Depression: America in the 1930s*, p. 203.

57. Quoted in Jeffers, *The Complete Idiot's Guide to the Great Depression*, p. 130.

Chapter Five: What Is the Legacy of the Great Depression?

58. Judy Busk, "Frugality: Legacy of the Great Depression," Always Lend a Helping Hand, New Deal Network. http://newdeal.feri.org.

59. Quoted in Tom Abbott, "Surviving the Depression: Advice from Interviewees," Always Lend a Helping Hand, New Deal Network. http://newdeal.feri.org.

60. Quoted in Abbott, "Surviving the Depression."

61. Lisa Nielsen, "A Hard Time," Always Lend a Helping Hand, New Deal Network. http://newdeal.feri.org.

62. Watkins, *The Great Depression: America in the 1930s*, p. 163.

63. Watkins, *The Great Depression: America in the 1930s*, p. 349.

64. Watkins, *The Great Depression: America in the 1930s*, p. 19.

Important People of the Great Depression

Hugh Hammond Bennett: Bennett founded and served as director of the Soil Conservation Service in 1935. He pioneered new methods of soil and water conservation and helped establish a series of soil erosion experiment stations to determine which crops, types of soil, and agricultural management practices did the most to conserve topsoil.

Calvin Coolidge: Coolidge was the thirtieth president of the United States, serving one term from 1924 to 1928. The period of happy days and easy money to be made during the 1920s was called "Coolidge Prosperity."

Herbert Hoover: Hoover succeeded Coolidge, becoming the thirty-first president of the United States. Hoover watched the stock market crash in October 1929, then did virtually nothing to help the floundering country during the next three years. His belated attempts to bring the country out of the Depression only worsened the situation. He was defeated in his bid for reelection in 1932 by Roosevelt.

Harry Hopkins: Hopkins was one of Roosevelt's closest advisers. He helped develop many New Deal programs, including the Works Progress Administration, which he directed. He also served as Roosevelt's unofficial ambassador to Great Britain in the early years of World War II.

Huey P. Long: Long served as governor of Louisiana from 1928 to 1932 and as a US Senator from 1932 to 1935, and many of his populist ideas became part of Roosevelt's New Deal programs. Nicknamed "The Kingfish," Long's extravagant style and almost dictatorial control of his state eventually made him the target of an assassin in 1935.

Charles E. Mitchell: Along with other Wall Street bankers, Mitchell (National City Bank chairman from 1921 to 1929) was initially hailed a hero for trying to forestall the stock market crash the week before Black Tuesday. He was arrested in 1933, indicted for income tax evasion, and exposed for unethical acts that contributed to the collapse of the stock market.

Ferdinand Pecora: Pecora led congressional hearings in 1933 to determine the causes of the stock market crash. Pecora's questioning of Wall Street bankers revealed unethical banking practices that contributed to the crash. Pecora was named a commissioner on the newly established Securities and Exchange Commission (SEC) in 1934.

Eleanor Roosevelt: Mrs. Roosevelt was America's First Lady from 1933 to 1945, a staunch supporter of her husband's New Deal policies and programs, and a pioneer in support of American civil rights legislation. After the death of her husband in 1945, she was appointed by President Harry Truman to be a delegate to the United Nations General Assembly and chaired the committee that drafted that body's Universal Declaration of Human Rights.

Franklin Delano Roosevelt: Roosevelt became the thirty-second president of the United States and was the only president elected to more than two terms. (Congress passed the Twenty-second Amendment, limiting presidents to two terms, in 1947. The Amendment was ratified in 1951.) He served from 1933 until his death during his fourth term of office—in 1945. His positive reassurance, evident in speeches and Fireside Chats, gave people hope during the Great Depression. His recovery program, the New Deal for the American People, helped pull the country out of it.

Shirley Temple: Temple, a child star with curly hair, dimples, and a winning smile, was America's sweetheart during the Great Depression. Starring in numerous movies during the mid-to-late 1930s, she helped take people's minds off their troubles during a time of national crisis.

For Further Research

Books

Cindy Barden and Maria Backus, *Industrialization Through the Great Depression*. Greensboro, NC: Carson-Dellosa/Mark Twain Media, 2011.

Jane Bingham, *The Great Depression: The Jazz Age, Prohibition, and the Great Depression, 1921–1937. A Cultural History of Women in America*. New York: Chelsea House, 2011.

Timothy Egan, *The Worst Hard Time: The Untold Story of Those Who Survived the Great American Dust Bowl*. New York: Houghton Mifflin, 2006.

Russell Freedman, *Children of the Great Depression*. New York: Clarion, 2005.

John Kenneth Galbraith, *The Great Crash, 1929*. Boston: Houghton Mifflin Harcourt, 2009. First published in 1955.

David E. Kyvig, *Daily Life in the United States, 1920–1940*. Chicago: Ivan R. Dee, 2004.

Melissa McDaniel, *The Great Depression*. New York: Children's, 2012.

Robert S. McElvaine, *The Great Depression: America, 1929–1941*. New York: Three Rivers, 2009.

Don Nardo, *Migrant Mother: How a Photograph Defined the Great Depression*. Mankato, MN: Compass Point, 2011.

Ronald A. Reis, *The Great Depression and the New Deal: America's Economy in Crisis*. New York: Chelsea House, 2011.

Movies

Dead End (1937). Directed by William Wyler, starring Joel McCrea, Humphrey Bogart, and Sylvia Sidney. Depicts inner-city life during the Great Depression. Described by a *New York Times* review as "disturbingly accurate."

The Grapes of Wrath (1940). Directed by John Ford, starring Henry Fonda, based on the novel of the same name by John Steinbeck. The story of the Joad family and how they migrated from their home in Oklahoma to California, seeking work and a better way of life. This movie is considered one of the best movies ever made and one of the best depictions of life during the Great Depression for those who lived in the Dust Bowl.

Sounder (1972). Directed by Martin Ritt, starring Cicely Tyson, Paul Winfield, and Kevin Hooks. The story of an African American family in Louisiana during the Great Depression. The movie emphasizes the plight of African Americans at the time.

Cinderella Man (2005). Directed by Ron Howard, starring Russell Crowe, Renée Zellweger, and Paul Giamatti. The story of James J. Braddock, a boxer in the late 1920s who goes from a title contender to a nobody because of an injury, leaving his family without support until he can heal and return to boxing for another chance at the title. The movie shows how close to disaster people lived during the Great Depression.

The Journey of Natty Gann (1985). Directed by Jeremy Kagan, starring Meredith Salenger and John Cusack. The story begins in Chicago, when Natty Gann leaves to find her father who had gone west to find work during the Great Depression. Based on the book of the same name by Ann Matthews.

Websites

American Experience: Surviving the Dust Bowl (www.pbs.org/wgbh /americanexperience/features/general-article/dustbowl-great-depres sion). An excellent website that contains the PBS documentary "Surviving the Dust Bowl" in video and transcript forms. Also included are numerous articles, interviews, biographies, photographs, and teaching guides and resources.

Digital History: The Great Depression (www.digitalhistory.uh.edu /modules/great_depression/index.cfm). This site contains primary resources, interviews, photographs, interviews, maps, historical newspapers, e-lectures, film trailers, flash movies, games, historical music, and an interactive timeline of events of the Great Depression.

History.com—The Great Depression (www.history.com/topics/great -depression). This excellent site contains over thirty links to articles on people, groups, themes, events, and topics relating to the Great Depression, along with photographs and videos.

Modern American Poetry: The Great Depression (www.english.ill inois.edu/maps/depression/depression.htm). Excellent information about the Great Depression and the Dust Bowl, with an extensive photo gallery and an extensive art gallery.

Wessels Living History Farm, York, Nebraska (www.livinghistory farm.org/farminginthe30s/farminginthe1930s.html). This site contains numerous video interviews with people who lived through the Great Depression. By clicking on any topic under "Farming in the 1930s," then clicking on one of the photos of people on the pages, the reader can hear each interview. Extensive information on farming during the 1930s.

Index

Picture Credits

About the Authors

Charles George and Linda George have been writing nonfiction books for children and teens since 1996. They live in West Texas and spend summers in Cloudcroft, New Mexico. *The Great Depression* is their sixty-eighth nonfiction book. Linda has also written five novels.